The myths and mythology of Ancient Egypt

The myths and mythology of Ancient Egypt

A comprehensive guide to the mysteries of creation, life and death

Lucia Gahlin

southwater

This edition is published by Southwater

Southwater is an imprint of
Anness Publishing Ltd
Hermes House, 88–89 Blackfriars Road
London SE1 8HA
tel. 020 7401 2077; fax 020 7633 9499
www.southwaterbooks.com
info@anness.com

© Anness Publishing Ltd 2003

This edition distributed in the UK
by The Manning Partnership Ltd
tel. 01225 478 444; fax 01225 478 440
sales@manning-partnership.co.uk

This edition distributed in the USA and
Canada by National Book Network
tel. 301 459 3366; fax 301 459 1705
www.nbnbooks.com

This edition distributed in Australia
by Pan Macmillan Australia
tel. 1300 135 113; fax 1300 135 103
customer.service@macmillan.com.au

This edition distributed in New Zealand
by The Five Mile Press (NZ) Ltd
tel. (09) 444 4144; fax (09) 444 4518
fivemilenz@clear.net.nz

A CIP catalogue record for this book is
available from the British Library.

Publisher: Joanna Lorenz
Managing Editor: Linda Fraser
Project Editor: Jennifer Schofield
Editorial Reader: Jay Thundercliffe
Production Controller: Joanna King
Designer: Jez MacBean
Jacket Design: Balley Design Associates
Picture Researcher: Veneta Bullen
Illustrator: Stuart Carter

Previously published as part of a larger
compendium, *Egypt: Gods, Myths and Religion*

1 2 3 4 5 6 7 8 9 10

CONTENTS

Ancient Egypt in Context

The key to Egypt's enduring stability and prosperity was the relationship between the pharaoh and the gods. The pharaoh was an absolute monarch who was believed to derive his power from the gods and who formed a link between them and the world of humankind. His mediating role was essential in maintaining the divine order that preserved the universe.

It was the pharaoh's duty to build temples and to ensure that offerings were made to the gods housed within them. In return, the gods would bestow blessings on the people, such as victory in battle, bountiful harvests and recovery from sickness. The Egyptian pantheon contained a vast number of gods and goddesses, each of whom might have several different forms or 'aspects', and the myths that concern them say much about the way in which the Egyptians perceived the divine world.

In his role as king, the pharaoh assumed divinity, but to some extent he was in fact a servant of the gods. It was the high priests who acted on behalf of the ruler in the great state temples erected throughout the country, which played a vital role in the structure of Egyptian civilization.

Introduction

▲ In this intimate scene decorating the side of Tutankhamun's small gold-plated shrine, the queen ties her husband's floral collar behind his neck. 18th Dynasty.

The civilization of the ancient Egyptians emerged about 5,000 years ago and continued to flourish for three millennia. Although it was not the oldest culture of the ancient world, it endured longer than any other, and in its heyday it was considered the most spectacular on Earth. Much of what we know about this remarkable society lay hidden for thousands of years, and some of its secrets are still being unearthed.

It was in the fertile areas around the great rivers of the Near East and North Africa that agriculture began, and with it came a settled, civilized human existence, which proceeded to bear rich cultural fruits. There is evidence of the existence of farming communities beside the Nile dating from c.5500 BC, and as these early settlements grew in sophistication, they each developed distinctive regional cultures, deities and myths.

When Egypt was unified in c.3100 BC, and ruled by a succession of pharaohs, the many local gods and goddesses that were worshipped, were not abandoned or suppressed. Instead, these deities became part of a vast and complex national pantheon. In some cases, the gods and goddesses underwent a process known as syncretism, in which their attributes were blended with those of another deity.

For administrative purposes, the country was still divided into a number of provinces, and each province had its own cult centre. The purpose of this cult centre was to serve the needs of the local gods and goddesses. The pharaoh, whose status lay somewhere between mortal and god, was regarded as an intermediary, and priestly ceremonies throughout Egypt were always carried out in his name. In return for this worship of the pharaoh, it was believed that the gods would protect his people.

The most important deities of the pantheon represented cosmic forces, and they and their myths helped to explain the great mysteries of life, such as birth and death, the rising and setting of the sun, and the return of the flood to the Nile each year.

Myths concerning the beginning of the world arose from each of the main cult centres throughout ancient Egypt and there were regional variations, each crediting the principal deity of the area with a leading role in creating, not only the other deities, but also with the creation of the universe.

Due to the fact that the ancient Egpytians were surrounded by the arid and life-threatening desert, they recognized their utter dependence on the regular revival of their agricultural land by the flooding of the Nile. They laid great emphasis on order, and an important theme that runs through Egyptian mythology was the maintenance of a settled way of life.

Egyptian beliefs about the afterlife also reflected their desire for order and continuity. Osiris, the benign god of fertility who was said to have taught humankind how to grow crops and build towns and temples, was also lord of the underworld and judge of the dead, who would ensure that life after death continued in the orderly manner the Egyptians enjoyed on earth. ◆

▼ The king was the only mortal who could be depicted face-to-face with a deity. Here Ramesses II encounters Amun. 19th Dynasty.

Timeline of Ancient Egypt

Before c.5500 BC

Early settlers in the Nile Valley; beginning of crop farming, growing wheat and barley.

c.5500–c.3100 BC
Predynastic and Protodynastic Period

Development of craftsmanship and animal husbandry.

Beginnings of social stratification.

Boats used on the Nile.

Construction using wattle and daub and beginning of mud brick.

Early wall painting and stone carving.

c.3100–c.2686 BC
Early Dynastic Period

Unification of Egypt.

Memphis established as capital.

Development of hieroglyphs.

c.2686–2181 BC
Old Kingdom

c.2650 BC

Step pyramid built at Saqqara during reign of Djoser.

c.2615 BC

Pyramid built at Meidum.

c.2580 BC

Great Pyramid at Giza built during reign of Khufu.

c.2530 BC

Great Sphinx built at Giza.

▶ *The Great Sphinx guards the Valley Temple of Khafre at Giza.*

c.2181–c.2055 BC
First Intermediate Period

Herakleopolitan and Theban dynasties control Egypt.

c.2055–c.1650 BC
Middle Kingdom

Egypt conquers Nubia, trades with Syria and Palestine.

Mudbrick pyramids built in Middle Egypt and at Dahshur.

Rock-cut tombs constructed in Middle Egypt.

c.1650–c.1550 BC
Second Intermediate Period

c.1600 BC

The horse is introduced into Egypt.

Hyksos claim control in Delta.

c.1550–c.1069 BC
New Kingdom

c.1550–c.1069 BC

Royal tombs built in the Valley of the Kings.

c.1348 BC

Akhenaten introduces worship of Aten, the sun disc, in place of established religion, and establishes a new capital, Akhetaten.

c.1336 BC

Capital moves back to Memphis.

c.1327 BC

Burial of King Tutankhamun in Valley of the Kings.

c.1250 BC

Ramesses II decorates the Hypostyle Hall at Karnak.

◀ *Nefertiti was the Chief Royal wife of the so-called "heretic" King Akhenaten. 18th Dynasty.*

c.1274 BC

Battle of Qadesh against the Hittites.

c.1209 BC

Egypt attacked by Mediterranean Sea Peoples.

c.1176 BC

Sea Peoples defeated by Ramesses III.

c.1069–c.747 BC
Third Intermediate Period

Egypt politically divided.

c.747–c.332 BC
Late Period

671 BC

Assyrians invade Egypt and reach Memphis.

525 BC

Egypt becomes part of the Persian Empire.

332BC–AD395
Ptolemaic and Roman Periods

332 BC

Egypt invaded by Alexander the Great, bringing it under Macedonian Greek rule. Alexandria founded.

305 BC

Ptolemy assumes power after death of Alexander.

30 BC

Egypt becomes part of the Roman Empire.

AD 324

Egypt adopts Christianity.

AD 395

End of Roman rule in Egypt.

The Land of Egypt

Ancient Egypt existed in a landscape of extremes, with vast expanses of arid desert bordering a narrow ribbon of wonderfully fertile land – and very little has changed to this day.

The Nile is Egypt's lifeblood. North of Aswan it flows for 900km (560 miles) through the Nile Valley until it reaches the Delta, which it traverses in a number of branches (five during the pharaonic period) before feeding its muddy water into the Mediterranean Sea. The silt it deposits is thick and black, inspiring the ancient Egyptians' name for their country, *Kemet* ('Black Land'). In contrast, the barren desert cliffs were seen to glow pink at dawn, so the desert was described as *Deshret* ('Red Land').

In ancient times, the Egyptian name for the summer season was *Akhet*, or Inundation. It was equivalent to the four months from July to October, when the great river overflowed its banks and flooded the Nile Valley and the Delta.

The huge volumes of water originated as rain that fell in central Sudan, raising the level of the White Nile. A few weeks later the summer monsoon rain falling over the Ethiopian highlands caused a very rapid swelling of the Blue Nile, and its tributary, the Atbara. All of these sources of water combined, reaching Egypt in a great swollen rush at the end of July.

Only in 1968 were the waters of the River Nile finally tamed, by the construction of the Aswan Dam. The Nile Valley is no longer flooded every year, and this has made a huge difference to Egypt's natural environment and way of life.

▲ *For most of the length of the Nile Valley, strips of fertile land border either side of the river, and the dividing line between desert and cultivation is clear-cut, as here at Tell el-Amarna.*

As well as providing ancient Egypt with, usually, two healthy harvests a year, the Nile was the principal means of transportation. It supplied much of the protein in the people's diet (in the form of fish and water birds). Ivory came from the tusks of the hippopotami that lived in the river, and papyrus was made from reeds that grew along its banks. Finally, the river was the source of mud, the chief ingredient of the most widely used building material – mudbricks. At the same time, the river could be treacherous: hippopotami, crocodiles, winds, currents, shallow waters and cataracts were all hazards that had to be taken seriously by the people whose lives depended on the Nile.

◄ *Scenes of agricultural life were commonly painted on the walls of private tombs. Here in their Theban tomb Sennedjem and his wife harvest their bountiful crops. c.1200 BC.*

The impregnable desert

The river was not the only place where danger lurked. The ancient Egyptians also particularly feared the desert. It was a place of searing heat by day and freezing cold by night, a waterless place of wild animals, fugitives and nomads. The desert dwellers often turned out to be marauders, and in addition there were countless demons who were supposed to live in the desert.

On the other hand, much of the greatness of the Egyptian civilization came from wealth yielded by the inhospitable desert. Its treasures included amethyst, turquoise, copper, limestone, sandstone, granite and – above all – gold. The desert lands also fulfilled another important function: they helped to make Egypt into an almost impregnable fortress. To either side of the Nile were the wastelands of the Eastern and Western, or Libyan, Deserts, to the north the Mediterranean Sea, and in the south was the first cataract of the Nile, which made the river unnavigable at that point. Egypt was protected from almost any outside threat. This resulted in an exceptionally stable society, and a strong sense of national identity flourished. A fear of the unknown resulted in a common mistrust of outsiders or foreigners (who were often described as *hesy*, meaning 'vile' or 'wretched').

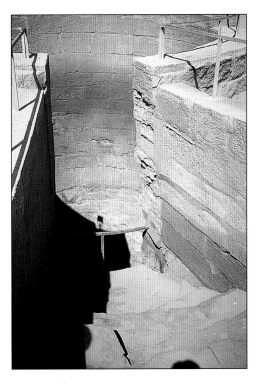

▶ *The copper inlay around the eyes of this painted statue from the 5th Dynasty represents the green malachite scribes wore to protect their eyes.*

Harnessing nature

The ancient Egyptians were self-sufficient in most things, except for suitable timber for building. The agricultural cycle revolved around the Nile flood, which could usually be depended on. Measuring gauges known as Nilometers were used to record the flood levels, so that suitable precautions might be taken if necessary. Efficient irrigation was crucial to agriculture. Farmers practised basin irrigation: they built earth banks to divide up areas of the flood plain, then led water into these artificial ponds and allowed it to stand before draining it off. The system could be administered on a local level.

The major crops were emmer wheat, barley and flax. Tomb scenes and models illustrate the various stages: ploughing, sowing the seed, harvesting, winnowing, threshing, and so on. Also depicted are the production of food and drink, such as grape-picking, wine pressing, brewing and breadmaking.

The dual benefits of the Nile and the sun made the land of Egypt a flourishing place. But as with all natural elements, there had to be precautions against their dangerous aspects. As protection against the overwhelming heat of the sun, people had to wear headcoverings to guard against sunstroke, and protected their eyes by wearing green malachite (copper) or black galena (lead) eye paints. Rain is not usually associated with Egypt, but it did occur in the north, and sometimes caused floods in the desert wadis; such problems had to be coped with. It therefore becomes clear that the lives of the ancient Egyptians were very much dictated by their natural environment and the climate. ◆

The Longest River

The Nile is the longest river in the world, flowing 6,741km (4,189 miles) from its source in the East African highlands to the Delta, a fertile area of about 22,000sq km (8,500sq miles). The Delta, named by the Greeks because it resembled the shape of the fourth letter of their alphabet, lies 17m (57ft) above sea level. Here the Nile once split into several channels before emerging into the Mediterranean Sea: of these only two now remain.

▲ *This Nilometer within the temple complex at Kom Ombo was constructed to gauge the river's rising level during the annual inundation.*

The Beginnings of Egyptian Civilization

Ancient Egypt as people usually imagine it – as the land of the pharaohs, with great temples, cities and burial sites, beautiful art and writing in hieroglyphs – came into being with the formation of a unified and centralized state in c.3100 BC. The factors that led to this development are speculative, but the most momentous changes in Egypt's history took place around 3000 BC.

For the first few hundred-thousand years of human occupation, Egypt was home to stone-age, or palaeolithic, hunting, fishing and food-gathering communities, which lived along the river terraces of the Nile Valley. Then, from c.5500 BC, the earliest agricultural communities emerged. Over the next 2,400 years, the country came to be divided between separate, self-governing communities, which developed at different rates socially, economically, politically and culturally. These early developments can be traced mainly by examining the so-called Predynastic burials, which have been excavated at various sites throughout Egypt.

Material culture

As the local cultures developed, their craftsmanship increased in quality and sophistication. Pottery was painted and jewellery fashioned; stone-working became more elaborate, with the manufacture of palettes, mace heads, knives and vases; metal-working began with the production of copper tools; and the copper ore malachite was used in the glaze for beads.

A recognizably Egyptian style was already beginning to emerge in the items being produced, and the markets for such goods clearly became wider and more specialized. Desert resources, such as gold from the Eastern Desert, were exploited and we know contact was made with traders from outside Egypt, as lapis lazuli from Badakhshan in north-eastern Afghanistan has been found in Predynastic graves.

The evidence of such artefacts indicates that their makers would have been freed from subsistence farming and that society was becoming differentiated, with the

◀ Celestial and bovine themes figure in what appears to be the earliest recorded religious imagery surviving from Egypt, such as on this Predynastic greywacke (slate) cosmetic palette.

▲ The ceremonial limestone 'Scorpion Macehead' from Hierakonpolis, shows King Scorpion of the Protodynastic Period engaged in an activity that may be the ritual cutting of an irrigation channel, or perhaps a foundation trench for a temple.

emergence of an elite who could afford luxury goods and who presumably controlled the trade routes, local irrigation systems and more elaborate building projects (especially tombs). Luxury goods may have been specially made to place in graves with the dead, and it seems that funerary customs played a major part in the increasing division of labour and the development of greater social complexity and stratification.

The exchange of goods would inevitably have been coupled with the exchange of ideas. The contact with Mesopotamia (modern Iraq) appears to have been particularly significant in the early period of Egyptian civilization. It is likely that foreign traders would have been attracted to Egypt by the prospect of purchasing its gold.

A centralized state emerges

By c.3100 BC, Egypt was a highly efficient political state, with an administrative bureaucracy, precisely defined boundaries and elaborate kingship rites relating to a single ruler. So why did the Egyptian state emerge when it did? There have been a number of theories, reflecting various trends in thought. They relate to changes in the physical environment and climate, as well as external stimuli. It is most likely that a variety of factors coincided to create the major changes.

▶ *The Protodynastic 'Two-dogs' ceremonial greywacke palette from Hierakonpolis is decorated with desert animals and two mythical long-necked beasts in the style of Mesopotamian art. The central circular area was for the grinding of pigments.*

Environmental changes are likely to have been tied in with a growth in the population, increased production, and the freeing of specialists from subsistence farming, resulting in the domination of the poor by an elite. It has been suggested that the growth in population caused the need for increased technology to meet the rising demand, which in turn resulted in the need for central organization. Other theories involve population growth leading to conflict between communities.

The increasing aridity of the desert over the millennia would have led to the narrowing of the area of habitable land, thus concentrating the population, and Egypt is known to have experienced a wetter period followed by a drier period around 3300 BC. The movement of people because of climatic changes (especially northwards into the Delta region) may well have caused both alliances and conflicts, resulting in the emergence of chiefdoms. Territorial competition and the merger of local chiefdoms no doubt led to increased power in the hands of fewer people.

Outside influences

Cultural transfer, especially from Mesopotamia and Elam, is often considered to have been the catalyst for Egypt's formation as a unified state, and the simultaneous emergence of a highly developed system of writing (hieroglyphics). But the direction and impact of any contact is still highly contested. Egypt's political superstructure was very likely well under way by the time western Asiatic motifs started to appear in Egyptian art. Examples show that the Egyptians made use of foreign ideas in a very Egyptian manner and soon chose to discard them.

While the development of writing helped to consolidate the unification of the state – aiding administrative efficiency and speeding up the processes of centralization of power – there is no evidence that Egyptian hieroglyphs had their origins in a foreign writing system. The beginnings of Egyptian civilization, often referred to as the Unification of Egypt, remain hazy and speculative. ◆

▲ *One of the designs most commonly found on Predynastic painted pots is that of a boat with cabins and banks of oars.*

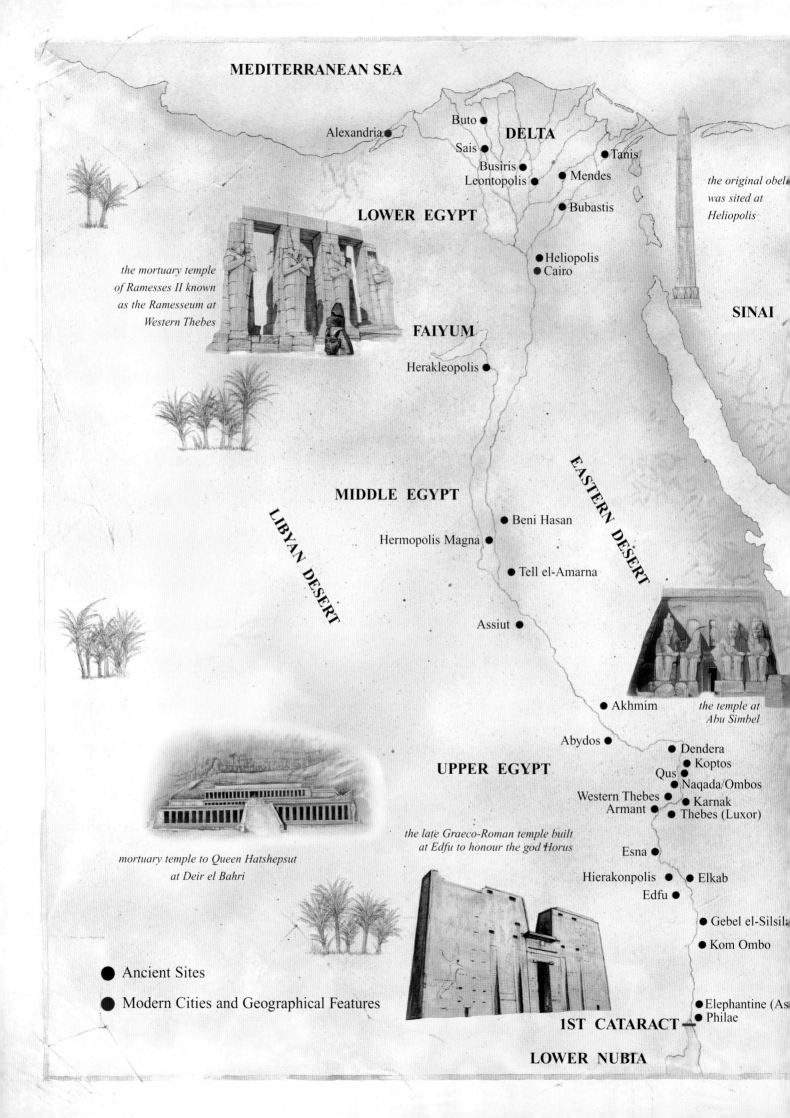

MEDITERRANEAN SEA

DELTA

Buto

Alexandria

Sais

Tanis

Busiris

Mendes

Leontopolis

LOWER EGYPT

Bubastis

*the original obel
was sited at
Heliopolis*

Heliopolis

Cairo

*the mortuary temple
of Ramesses II known
as the Ramesseum at
Western Thebes*

SINAI

FAIYUM

Herakleopolis

MIDDLE EGYPT

EASTERN DESERT

Beni Hasan

LIBYAN DESERT

Hermopolis Magna

Tell el-Amarna

Assiut

*the temple at
Abu Simbel*

Akhmim

Abydos

UPPER EGYPT

Dendera

Koptos

Qus

Naqada/Ombos

Western Thebes

Karnak

Armant

Thebes (Luxor)

*mortuary temple to Queen Hatshepsut
at Deir el Bahri*

*the late Graeco-Roman temple built
at Edfu to honour the god Horus*

Esna

Hierakonpolis

Elkab

Edfu

Gebel el-Silsila

Kom Ombo

● Ancient Sites

● Modern Cities and Geographical Features

Elephantine (As

Philae

1ST CATARACT

LOWER NUBIA

Main Cult Centres

The Nile river and the narrow, fertile band of arable land along its length has always supported the population of Egypt. It was along the banks of the Nile that people first settled. These settlements developed into sophisticated communities, with their own administrative centres, ruling bodies, temples, priesthoods and deities. The gods and goddesses that the local people chose to worship were initially peculiar to each location, although as society evolved and the links between the townships developed, the same gods frequently appear to have been worshipped in more than one centre. The existence of a deity helped to explain the creation of humankind, and other natural phenomena. The gods were beneficent, offering protection against war and famine in return for reverence and worship. The most well-known cult centres are indicated on the map with a red spot.

NORTH

RED SEA

Gods and Goddesses

The ancient Egyptians worshipped a multitude of gods and goddesses, and an understanding of these is crucial for any enquiry into Egyptian mythology and religion. It is, however, easy to be baffled by the great number of deities, the variety of forms they take and the complexity of the relationships between them.

The Egyptians inhabited a natural environment that could prove hazardous and life was unpredictable. Much of what they encountered in life and the world around them may have seemed mysterious and incomprehensible. The gods and goddesses they conjured up were divine personifications of all that was important to them, particularly in maintaining a sense of order and well-being in this life and the next, ensuring the survival of the next generation and the continued fertility of the soil. So there were, for example, gods of the cosmos, the afterlife, childbirth, grain, even drunkenness and merriment. The stories or myths that evolved around the various gods and goddesses were a means of explaining the unknown, such as why it was dark at night, or the cause of an illness.

Worship often involved making offerings to the gods accompanied by invocation, in order to ensure their continued and benign presence in the lives of the people.

◀ *Ancient Egyptian deities were represented in a variety of forms. Here at Karnak the god Amun appears as ram-headed sphinxes guarding the processional way to his temple.*

Divine Forms

Religion was central to the lives of the ancient Egyptians, and central to their religion were the gods and goddesses they worshipped. They were the protagonists in the religious texts, and in the temple and tomb scenes that survive from Egypt's past. Each had their own distinctive characteristics and identities.

The ancient Egyptians appear to have had no single sacred book into which their ideas and beliefs were consolidated. Among the extant religious treatises there is no one divine explanation as to the origins of humankind and the universe, but several which seem to contradict one another. Each of the main cult centres of Egypt had its own version of the story centred around a different creator god, but it is impossible to know which one was most widely believed at any one time. The diversity of these creation myths serves to emphasize the interconnected and yet seemingly contradictory system of beliefs referred to as

▶ Bastet was often represented as a cat, but could also appear as a woman with a feline head. Her statues are often adorned with jewellery. The bronze 'Gayer Anderson cat' has silver inlays and gold earrings and nose ring. 30 BC.

ancient Egyptian religion. Various sources reveal the extreme complexity of the representations and interrelationships of the gods and goddesses.

Thoth, for example, was a lunar deity; he was also the god of wisdom and of scribes. He was often represented as a man with the head of an ibis, or entirely in the form of this bird, but he could also be depicted as a baboon. Horus, on the other hand, is always found in partial or complete falcon configuration (not to be confused with the Theban god of warfare Montu, who was also depicted in this way) but on some occasions his mother is said to be the goddess Hathor, whereas at other times she is said to be the goddess Isis. Seemingly distinct deities may actually be incarnations of the same one; for example, Bastet, the mother goddess in cat form, appears to be the more gentle embodiment of the aggressive Sekhmet, the lioness goddess whose name translates as 'the powerful one'.

So we see that in the imaginations of the Egyptians, the gods fused human and animal elements. Greater

◀ This scribe from the ancient city of Akhetaten sits cross-legged before Thoth, represented here as a baboon. The god's headdress bears both the full and the crescent moon, indicating his lunar association. 18th Dynasty.

accessibility might have been achieved by representing deities in male and female human form, but a sense of mystery was instilled by the combination with animal form. It is interesting, however, that divine personifications of the environment or the cosmos, such as Geb, the god of the earth, or Hapy, god of the Nile inundation, tend to be given human form. Even when deities are represented partially or totally as animals, they exhibit human behaviour and express human emotions, haranguing each other in court for example, or getting drunk and falling asleep.

Gods in animal form

The attributes and behaviour of an animal clearly determined its selection as the representation of a deity. For example, the fierce goddess Sekhmet takes the form of a ferocious lioness and Khepri, god of the sun and creation, is represented as a dung beetle, which has

► *Taweret's sagging breasts and large rounded stomach identified her with pregnant women and mothers.*

the habit of rolling its eggs in a ball of dung. Another consideration appears to have been that, by depicting a deity in the form of a dangerous animal such as a snake (for example, the fertility goddess Renenutet or Mertseger, the patron deity of the west Theban peak), and then by worshipping that deity, the animal in question might in turn be placated and the hazard allayed.

Sometimes the form particular deities were given must also have been apotropaic (able to ward off harm). Take, for example, the protective goddess of

childbirth, Taweret, who is portrayed as a hippopotamus with additional characteristics of a crocodile and a lion. The idea was that such a potentially threatening combination would keep harm away from mother and child.

The concept of a composite animal is most clearly exemplified by the demon deity, Ammit, who was responsible for devouring the hearts of those who had done wrong during their lifetime, thereby denying them a life after death. She was represented as part crocodile, part lion or panther, and part hippopotamus. The ancient Egyptians clearly dreamt up strange combinations of animals in order to represent the more menacing of divine forces.

All the animals in the collective visualization of the divine world were indigenous to the Nile Valley, the marshy Delta region and the desert fringes. Though the giraffe was known to exist, because it had been brought into Egypt as an example of exotica from sub-Saharan Africa; it was never chosen to represent a deity. There is, however, one god whose animal form remains a mystery, and that is Seth. Perhaps due to his association with chaos and infertility, he was depicted as an animal with a forked tail, a greyhound-like body, a long snout and squared-off ears. Either such a beast did not actually exist, or it is long extinct.

The significance of names

Perhaps by visualizing and verbalizing the divine world in terms of customary animals and routine human behaviour, the intention was to demystify and make explicable what was by definition mysterious and incomprehensible. Nevertheless, divinity can never be fully understood and must instil a sense of wonder in the non-divine. In the myth of *Isis and the Sun God's Secret Name*, it is the one unknown name of Re that is the source of his power; the hidden essence

is crucial. The names of the deities were decidedly as important as their particular characteristics and the means by which they were represented. Offerings and prayers could be made only to a divine force that had its own name.

Myths served to explain the origins, personalities and relationships of the deities, but it is impossible to know for certain how and when the identities of the gods and goddesses of ancient Egypt evolved. All we can do is identify the earliest known occurrence of the deity in each instance (whether a representation or textual reference). It is likely that the priesthood formulated and developed the various theological ideas associated with the gods and goddesses. ◆

▼ *Hapy, the god of the Nile inundation, was portrayed with rolls of fat and heavy breasts, emphasizing his connection with fecundity. This image, symbolizing the Unification of Egypt exemplifies the ancient Egyptians' love of symmetry in art.*

Deities and Cult Centres

During the Dynastic Period of Egyptian history, from the formation of the state of Egypt in c.3100 BC through to the conquest of Egypt by Alexander the Great in 332 BC, Egypt was divided into administrative districts, called nomes, each with its own capital. There were 22 nomes in the Nile Valley (Upper Egypt) and twenty in the Delta region (Lower Egypt). They probably reflected the composition of the separate chiefdoms of the Predynastic Period, before the unification of Egypt under one king. Each nome had its own cult centre, with a priesthood to service the needs of the local deity (or *njwty*, from the ancient Egyptian *niwt* meaning city), and a temple with a shrine for the residence of the god or goddess.

In fact, each cult centre tended to house not a sole deity but a whole divine family or triad, such as Ptah, Sekhmet and Nefertem at Memphis, or Osiris, Isis and Horus at Abydos.

Sometimes, an extended family tree of gods and goddesses can be traced, such as that connected with the cult centre of Heliopolis (see *Creation Myths*). There might also be a mythological link between deities associated with temples some distance apart. For example Hathor of Dendera and Horus of Edfu were united on certain festival days, when Hathor was said to make an annual voyage to Edfu to be united with Horus.

A division of deities into more manageable genealogies would have been necessary for the ordering of such a multitude of divine beings. A survey of these groupings, however, soon reveals overlaps; Amun ('the Hidden One'), for example, occurs in both the triad of Thebes and the Ogdoad (eight gods) of Hermopolis. This does not appear to have troubled the ancient Egyptians. Theirs was an add-on religion, from

Egyptian economy

The administrators of Egypt's forty-two nomes were responsible for the collection of taxes on behalf of the central government. Most people were subsistence farmers and much of the local economy was based on bartering. Taxes were collected in the form of grain, meat, minerals and other goods. The tax system was the responsibility of the king's vizier, or chief minister.

The agrarian system also came under the supervision of the nome administrators, who registered landowners. The total yield of grain in any one year largely depended on the amount of land that could be cultivated as a result of the annual inundation. Irrigation systems were developed to extend this area as far as possible, and it was in the interests of the authorities to see that they were kept in good condition.

◄ *This statue of Horus stands at the entrance to the Hypostyle Hall in the temple of Edfu. As the god of kingship, the falcon deity wears the Double Crown of Upper and Lower Egypt.*

which ideas were never discarded in favour of new ones; instead a cumulative effect can be seen, and in fact the antiquity of any religious element heightened its sacredness.

Politics

The development of the state religion was heavily influenced by political factors. A local deity might rise to national importance because he or she shared a home town with a new ruling family, such as the Eleventh and Eighteenth Dynasties, whose capital was Thebes. Their conquests and claiming of the throne resulted in the prominence of the gods Montu and Amun.

Political motives might also be responsible for the fusion of two deities into one (a process known as syncretism). An example is Amun-Re, head of the pantheon during the New Kingdom (c.1550–c.1069 BC). He was a combination of Amun the patron deity of Thebes, by then the religious capital of the whole of Egypt, and the ancient sun god Re, whose cult at Heliopolis was one of the oldest and whose priesthood had always had particular influence. This union was probably the result of a political alliance.

The degree to which politics and religious belief could interact became

◄ *Amun can often be identified by his double-plumed headdress. Here he sits behind a figure of Tutankhamun. 18th Dynasty.*

▲ *Akhenaten attempted to abolish the traditional polytheistic religion. Here he is shown offering lotus flowers to his sole god, Aten, represented as the sun's disc. 18th Dynasty.*

even more apparent during the reign of the Eighteenth-Dynasty king Akhenaten (c.1352–c.1336 BC), when he abandoned Thebes to found a new capital, Akhetaten. Here he tried to establish a new religion, erasing the inscriptions to Amun and the other traditional gods and recognizing only one deity, the Aten. Akhenaten's actions may have been an attempt to curb the political power of Amun's priests, but his reforms failed, possibly because they were not welcomed by most Egyptians, who clung to the rich complexity of strongly personalized deities to whom they could relate directly. ◆

Deification of Mortals

It was rare but not unheard of for the ancient Egyptians to deify eminent individuals from the past. The king himself was considered a god to some extent, particularly after his death, but occasionally a local cult might grow up around a ruler in addition to his official funerary cult, and he would be worshipped as a patron deity in a more unusual way. The most popular was Amenhotep I (c.1525–c.1504 BC), the second ruler of the Eighteenth Dynasty. Together with his mother, Ahmose-Nefertari, he was worshipped as a protective deity and founder of Deir el-Medina, the west Theban village of tomb builders. He was treated like the patron saint of this small workmen's community. There was a shrine dedicated to him, festivals were

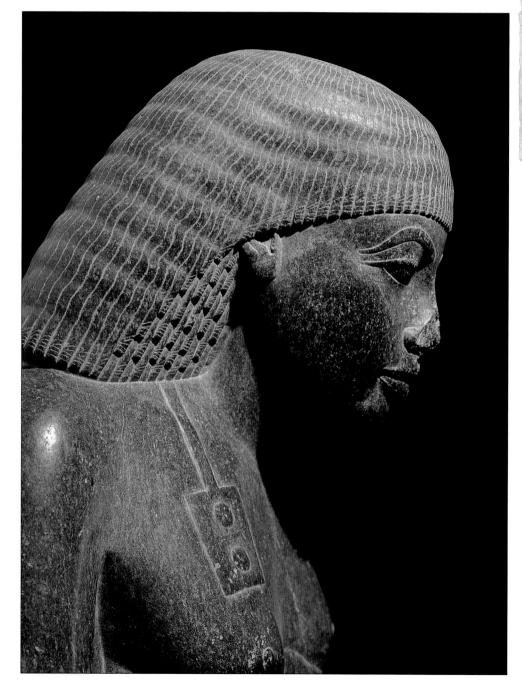

Imhotep's Pyramid

The Step Pyramid at Saqqara was built c.2650 for the burial of the Third-Dynasty king Djoser. The building began as a mastaba tomb (a superstructure named from the Arabic word for 'bench'). This was then extended in size and three further levels were erected over it to form a four-step pyramid. Finally, it was enlarged again and two further steps were added.

The base of the pyramid measures 140 x 118m (459 x 387ft) and it is 60m (197ft) high. At the time of its construction it was by far the largest monument in Egypt, and was also the first to be built from blocks of limestone rather than mudbrick. It was surrounded by a funerary complex for the king, containing mortuary temples and a statue chamber within a walled enclosure.

celebrated in his honour, and sometimes his statue was carried by priests so that his oracle might be consulted.

The best-known non-royal figures who were posthumously honoured with deification were Imhotep and Amenhotep son of Hapu, but from the New Kingdom onwards (c.1550 BC) victims of drowning began to be deified. The River Nile was the lifeline of the ancient Egyptian people and much religious belief surrounded it. By the Late Period a person who had drowned in it might sometimes have a cult established in their honour.

Imhotep

The great vizier, or chief minister, of the Third-Dynasty king Djoser (c.2667–c.2648 BC), Imhotep was the architect of Egypt's earliest monumental stone structure, the Step Pyramid Complex of Djoser at Saqqara, the chief

◀ *Amenhotep son of Hapu is shown here with his scribal palette hanging over his shoulder, loaded with two circular cakes of red and black ink. 18th Dynasty.*

for deification, hence the connection between the cults of Imhotep and the Egyptian god of wisdom, Thoth. Healing sanctuaries were dedicated to Imhotep, one of which was built within the confines of the ruler Hatshepsut's Eighteenth-Dynasty mortuary temple at Deir el-Bahri on the west bank of the Nile at Thebes. It was in sanatoriums such as this one that the ancient Egyptians of the first millennium BC indulged in the practice known as incubation. They slept in the sanatorium in the hope of receiving from the deity in question a helpful or healing dream (particularly concerning fertility problems).

Imhotep came to be regarded as the son of the chief god of Memphis, Ptah. Many bronze statuettes represent him wearing a skull cap (like Ptah), and a priest's long linen kilt, seated with a papyrus scroll rolled out across his lap.

Amenhotep son of Hapu

The Deir el-Bahri sanctuary was also dedicated to another god of healing, the second deified sage, Amenhotep son of Hapu, who had been an important official during the reign of the Eighteenth-Dynasty king Amenhotep III (c.1390–c.1352 BC). Like Imhotep he was remembered for his wisdom, and as Director of Royal Works he was also responsible for building a great funerary structure for

▶ *Imhotep was a favourite subject for bronze figurines during the Late and Graeco-Roman Periods. He sits here with a papyrus scroll stretched across his lap.*

his king. This was the west Theban mortuary temple of Amenhotep III at Kom el-Heiten. Amenhotep son of Hapu was granted the unique royal favour of his own mortuary temple among those of the kings at Thebes, and statues of him were set up in the largest and most influential temple of the time, that of Amun at Karnak on the east bank at Thebes. ◆

▲ *Amenhotep I and his mother, Ahmose Nefertari, were worshipped as patron deities of Deir el-Medina long after their deaths. 18th Dynasty.*

burial site at the time for the capital at Memphis. An inscription on a statue of the king honours his vizier as a master carpenter and sculptor, while carvings on stone vessels say that he was a priest.

Imhotep was obviously remembered throughout pharaonic history, but he was not actually deified until the Late Period, some 2,000 years after his death. In fact he was particularly acknowledged during the Ptolemaic Period (332–30 BC), when he was identified with the Greek Asklepios as a god of wisdom and medicine. A reputation for great wisdom does appear to have been a prerequisite

The Deities

The ancient Egyptian gods and goddesses could take many different human and animal forms; Thoth, for example, could be depicted as a baboon, an ibis; or a man with the head of an ibis. Many of the deities would have been worshipped in temples and shrines throughout Egypt, but only their cult centres best known today are listed below. All aspects of life in the human world were reflected in the divine world and the range of associations held by the deities and goddesses listed below show this.

▶ *Hathor was depicted as a cow leaving the desert to come to the papyrus marshes. 19th Dynasty.*

GOD/GODDESS	APPEARANCE	MAIN CULT CENTRE(S)	ASSOCIATION(S)/ROLE
Aker (god)	Two lions back-to-back; tract of land with lion or human heads at either end		Earth; east & west horizons in Underworld
Amaunet (goddess)	Snake-headed	Hermopolis Magna	Primeval; hidden power
Amenhotep Son of Hapu (god)	Man	Thebes	Healing
Ammit (goddess)	Head of crocodile; front part of panther or lion; rear of hippopotamus	Thebes	Devourer of heart at Judgement
Amun (god)	Man with double-plumed headdress; ram or ram-headed; goose; frog-headed	Thebes; Hermopolis Magna	'King of gods'; primeval; hidden power
Anat (goddess)	Woman with lance, axe & shield		War; Syria-Palestinian
Anubis (god)	Jackal or jackal-headed		Cemeteries; embalming
Anuket/Anukis (goddess)	Woman with tall plumed headdress & papyrus sceptre	Elephantine	Cataracts; huntress
Apis (god)	Bull	Memphis	Manifestation of Ptah
Apophis (god)	Snake		Underworld; chaos; enemy of sun god
Arensnuphis (god)	Man with plumed crown	includ. Philae	Nubian
Astarte (goddess)	Naked woman with *Atef*-crown or bull's horns, riding horse		War; Syrian
Aten (god)	Sun disc	Akhetaten	Solar
Atum (god)	Man with *Nemes* headdress or Double Crown; snake	Heliopolis	'Totality'; creator; solar
Baal (god)	Man with pointed beard & horned helmet, holding a cedar tree, club or spear		Sky; storms; Syrian (Ugaritic)
Baba (god)	Baboon		Aggression; virility; penis = bolt of heaven's doors or mast of Underworld boat

GOD/GODDESS	APPEARANCE	MAIN CULT CENTRE(S)	ASSOCIATION(S)/ROLE
Banebdjedet (god)	Ram	Mendes	Virility; sky
Bastet (goddess)	Cat or cat-headed	Bubastis	Daughter; 'Eye of Re'
Bat (goddess)	Human head with cow's ears & horns, & body in shape of necklace counterpoise	Upper Egypt	Celestial; fertility
Benu (god)	Heron	Heliopolis	Solar; rebirth
Bes (god)	Leonine dwarf		Household; childbirth
Buchis (god)	Bull	Armant	Manifestation of Re & Osiris
Duamutef (god)	Jackal-headed		Canopic; stomach & upper intestines; east
Geb (god)	Man (smtms ithyphallic), smtms with goose on head or Red Crown	Heliopolis	Earth; fertility
Hapy (god)	Man with pendulous breasts & aquatic plants headdress	Gebel el-Silsila; Aswan	Nile inundation
Hapy (god)	Baboon-headed		Canopic; lungs; north
Hathor (goddess)	Cow; woman with cow ears, or horns and sun disc on head, or falcon on perch on head	Dendera; Deir el-Bahri	Mother (esp. of king); love; fertility; sexuality; music; dance; alcohol; sky; Byblos; turquoise; faience
Hatmehyt (goddess)	Lepidotus fish	Mendes	
Hauhet (goddess)	Snake-headed	Hermopolis Magna	Primeval; formlessness; flood force
Heket (goddess)	Frog or frog-headed	Qus	Childbirth
Herishef (god)	Long-horned ram with Atef-crown & sun-disc headdress	Herakleopolis	Primeval force; creator; solar
Horus (god)	Falcon or falcon-headed	Edfu; Hierakonpolis; Behdet	Sky; kingship
Hu (god)	Man		Divine utterance; authority
Huh/Heh (god)	Frog-headed; man holding notched palm-rib	Hermopolis Magna	Primeval; formlessness; flood force; infinity
Ihy (god)	Child	Dendera	Sistrum (rattle)
Imhotep (god)	Seated man with skull cap & papyrus roll	Memphis; Thebes	Wisdom; medicine
Ipy/Ipet (goddess)	Hippopotamus	Thebes	Magical protection
Ishtar (goddess)	Woman		Astral; 'lady of battle'; sexuality; fertility; healing; Assyrian
Isis (goddess)	Woman with throne headdress	includ. Philae	Mother (of king); magic
Imsety (god)	Human-headed		Canopic; liver; south
Kauket (goddess)	Snake-headed	Hermopolis Magna	Primeval; darkness
Khepri (god)	Scarab beetle or man with scarab beetle for head		Creator; solar
Khnum (god)	Ram or ram-headed	Elephantine; Esna	Creator; potter; cataract; fertile soil
Khons(u) (god)	Child with headdress of full and crescent moon	Thebes	Moon
Kuk (god)	Frog-headed	Hermopolis Magna	Primeval; darkness
Maat (goddess)	Woman with single feather headdress		Order, truth, justice
Mafdet (goddess)	Woman; panther		Protector against snakes & scorpions
Mandulis (god)	Man with headdress of ram horns, plumes, sun-discs & cobras	Kalabsha; Philae	Solar; Lower Nubian
Mehen (god)	Coiled serpent		Protector of sun god

GOD/GODDESS	APPEARANCE	MAIN CULT CENTRE(S)	ASSOCIATION(S)/ROLE
Mehet-Weret (goddess)	Cow		Sky; primordial waters; 'great flood'
Mer(e)tseger (goddess)	Cobra	Western Thebes	'Peak of the West'; 'she who loves silence'
Meskhen(e)t (goddess)	Brick with human head; woman with bicornate uterus headdress		Childbirth; destiny
Mihos (god)	Lion	Leontopolis; Bubastis	
Min (god)	Man with erect phallus, & double-plumed headdress	Koptos; Akhmim	Fertility; mining regions in Eastern Desert
Mnevis (god)	Bull	Heliopolis	Sacred bull of sun god; oracles
Montu (god)	Falcon or falcon-headed, with sun disc & double-plumed headdress	Thebes	War
Mut (goddess)	Vulture	Thebes	Motherhood
Naunet (goddess)	Snake-headed	Hermopolis Magna	Primordial waters
Nefertem (god)	Man with lotus headdress; lion-headed	Memphis; Buto	Primeval lotus blossom
Neith (goddess)	Woman with Red Crown of Lower Egypt holding shield & crossed arrows	Sais	Creator-goddess; warfare; weaving
Nekhbet (goddess)	Vulture	el-Kab	Tutelary goddess of Upper Egypt
Neper (god)	Man		Grain
Nephthys (goddess)	Woman with headdress of a basket & enclosure		Funerary; protective
Nun (god)	Man; holding solar barque above head; frog-headed; baboon	Heliopolis; Hermopolis Magna	Primordial waters
Nut (goddess)	Woman; cow	Heliopolis	Sky; sarcophagus
Onuris (god)	Man; beard; four plume headdress;	This	Warrior/hunter carrying spear
Osiris (god)	Mummified man with *Atef*-crown, holding crook & flail	Abydos; Busiris	Death; Afterlife; rebirth; fertility; agriculture
Pakhet (goddess)	Lioness	Includ. entrance to wadi in E. desert nr Beni Hasan	
Ptah (god)	Semi-mummified man with skull cap and *was-djed-ankh* sceptre	Memphis	Creator; craftsmen
Qadesh (goddess)	Naked woman standing on lion		Sacred ecstasy; sexual pleasure; Middle Eastern
Qebehsenuef (god)	Falcon-headed		Canopic; lower intestines; west
Re/Ra (god)	Ram- or falcon-headed with sun disc & cobra headdress	Heliopolis	Creator; solar
Renenutet (goddess)	Cobra	Faiyum	Harvest; nursing
Reshef/Reshep (god)	Man with beard & White Crown with gazelle head at front & ribbon behind		War; Syrian (Amorite)
Sah (god)	Man		Orion
Satet/Satis (goddess)	Woman with White Crown & antelope horns	Elephantine	Protectoress of southern border; fertility
Sekhmet (goddess)	Lioness or lioness-headed	Memphis	'Powerful'; daughter of Re; healing
Selket/Serket (goddess)	Woman with scorpion headdress		Funerary; protective
Seshat (goddess)	Woman with panther-skin robe, & seven-pointed star on head		Writing

GOD/GODDESS	APPEARANCE	MAIN CULT CENTRE(S)	ASSOCIATION(S)/ROLE
Seth (god)	Unidentified quadruped or 'Seth-animal' headed	Ombos Naqada	Chaos; infertility; desert; storm
Shay (god)	Man		Destiny
Shezmu (god)	Man	Faiyum	Underworld demon; wine & unguent-oil presses
Shu (god)	Man with feather on head; lion-headed	Heliopolis; Leontopolis	Air; 'Eye of Re'
Sia (god)	Man		Divine knowledge; intellectual achievement
Sobek (god)	Crocodile or crocodile-headed	Kom Ombo; Faiyum	Pharaonic might
Sokar (god)	Mummified man with crown of horns, cobras, *atef*, & sun disc; hawk-headed	Memphis	Funerary
Sopdet/Sothis (goddess)	Woman with star on head		'Dog star' Sirius
Tatenen (god)	Man with double-plumed crown & ram's horns	Memphis	Emerging Nile silt from receding flood waters; vegetation
Taweret (goddess)	Hippopotamus (with lion & crocodile parts)		Household; childbirth
Tayet (goddess)	Woman		Weaving
Tefnut (goddess)	Woman; lioness-headed; cobra	Heliopolis; Leontopolis	Moisture; 'Eye of Re'; *uraeus*
Thoth/Djehuty (god)	Baboon; ibis or ibis-headed	Hermopolis Magna	Moon; knowledge; scribes
Wadjet/Edjo (goddess)	Cobra; lioness	Buto	Tutelary goddess of Lower Egypt; *uraeus*
Wepwawet (god)	Jackal or jackal-headed	Assiut	'Opener of the Ways'

▲ The goddess Neith was associated with warfare. 25th Dynasty.

▲ The goddess Nut continued to be represented inside coffins well into the Roman period in Egypt. Early 2nd century AD.

▲ The goddess Maat, the divine personification of truth, order and justice, wore an ostrich feather on her head. 19th Dynasty.

27

Headdresses and Crowns

An incredible variety of crowns and headdresses are represented in the art of ancient Egypt. For those who are unable to read the hieroglyphic inscriptions which often accompany the depictions of gods and goddesses, the headdress can be crucial for identifying a particular deity. Some of the characteristics of divine headdresses include: feathers; horns, lunar and solar discs; various birds, insects and other creatures; stars; a notched palm frond; a pot; a lotus flower; a shield with crossed arrows; a throne; and so on. The king might be depicted wearing one of several different crowns, although he was often shown wearing the simple linen *nemes* (headcloth). Various deities could also be portrayed wearing a royal headdress, for example Osiris who often sported the *Atef*-crown. The Blue Crown was especially associated with warfare.

White Crown of Upper Egypt (*hedjet*)

Red Crown of Lower Egypt (*deshret*)

Double Crown of Upper and Lower Egypt (*pschent*)

Atef crown

Blue Crown (*khepresh*)

Tatenen

Wadjet/Edjo

Thoth

Isis

Nephthys

Re

Neith

Buchis

Nefertem

Neith

Meskhent

Bes

Heh

Nut

Renenutet

▲ *Identification of this Nile deity by Itis head-dress is especiallly useful when late period bronze figurines such as this one are uninscribed.*

Selket/Serket

 Khepri

 Montu

 Maat, Shu

 Atum, Horus

▲ *The elongated headdress is characteristic of 'Amarna Art'. Here Akhenaten's headdress is surmounted by ram's horns, a sun disc, and the tall plumes. 18th Dynasty.*

 Osiris

 Neith

 Nekhbet, Mut, Isis

Hathor, Isis, Ipy/Ipet

Mandulis

Seshat

Khnum

Sobek

Re-Horakhty, Sekhmet, Sokar

 Geb

 Hathor

 Khons

▲ *Osorkon II as Osiris, flanked by Horus and Isis, wear characteristic headdresses. Isis is also often shown with a throne on her head. 22nd Dynasty.*

 Satet/Satis

Reshef/Reshep

Amun, Horus, Min

 Onuris

Anuket/Anukis

 Sopdet/Sothis

 Geb

Gods and Goddesses

The Egyptian pantheon included hundreds of deities: many originated as local gods who became the focus of important cults, while some were borrowed from other cultures. Some deities were merged, or 'syncretized' with each other, blending their attributes, sometimes allowing a lesser god to take on the distinction and importance of a greater one. Most of the major, or universal, deities represented cosmic forces, such as the sun or the flood, or were associated with the mysteries of human life, such as birth and death.

Aker

The earth god Aker was the divine personification of the eastern and western horizons, which signified the entrance and exit into and out of the Netherworld, Aker was important in funerary texts and imagery. He was represented as two lions sitting back to back, or as a piece of land with a lion or a human head at each end (one facing east and one facing west).

Amun

By the New Kingdom (c.1550–c.1069 BC) Amun had achieved the position of head of the state pantheon. His national significance was due to the emergence of local Theban rulers who were successful in reuniting and ruling the whole of Egypt after a period of disruption. An early Twelfth-Dynasty inscription in the jubilee chapel of King Senusret I (c.1965–c.1920 BC) at Karnak describes Amun as 'the king of the gods'. His pre-eminence also had much to do with his amalgamation with Re, the ancient sun god of Heliopolis, to create the deity Amun-Re. He was also combined with the fertility god Min, to form the god Amun-Min or Amun Kamutef ('Bull of his Mother').

Amun's name means 'the Hidden One' and one of his epithets was 'mysterious of form', although he was usually

represented in human form wearing a tall double-plumed headdress. He could also be envisaged as a ram – *Ovis platyra* – with horns curving inwards close to the head. In a hymn on Papyrus Leiden 1,350, he is described as the 'Great Honker' – a primeval goose.

From at least as early as the Eleventh Dynasty (c.2055 – c.1985 BC) Amun's chief cult centre was the temple at Karnak in Thebes, where he was worshipped with his consort, the vulture mother-goddess Mut, and their child the lunar deity Khonsu. As early as the Fifth Dynasty (c.2350–c.2345 BC) he appeared in the Pyramid Texts accompanied by a consort named as Amaunet.

Anat

As a goddess of war, Anat was believed to protect the king in battle. Thus she was often depicted with a lance, axe and shield. She also wore a tall crown surmounted by feathers.

Anat is an excellent example of the Egyptian acceptance of foreign deities into their pantheon of gods, because she actually originated in Syria-Palestine as

▲ *Above the backs of the two lions representing Aker, the artist of this papyrus Book of the Dead of Ani has painted the hieroglyphic signs for 'horizon' (*akhet*) and 'sky' (*pet*).*

▼ *In reliefs at Luxor the supreme god Amun takes an ithyphallic form as Amun Kamutef.*

▲ *These ram-headed sphinxes (criosphinxes) originally formed part of the avenue between the temples of Luxor and Karnak. Both were dedicated to the god Amun, who was sometimes represented as a ram.*

a deity of the Canaanites and Phoenicians. She was said to be the sister, or sometimes the consort, of Baal. There is evidence of a cult dedicated to her in Egypt from at least the late Middle Kingdom (c.1800 BC).

Like other more benign goddesses, Anat held the titles 'Mother of All the Gods' and 'Mistress of the Sky'. At various times she was regarded as the consort of Seth or the fertility god Min.

Anubis

The god of embalming and cemeteries, Anubis was an ancient deity to whom prayers for the survival of the deceased in the Afterlife were addressed during the early Old Kingdom before Osiris rose to prominence as the god of the dead. Anubis continued to assist in the judgement of the dead and accompanied the deceased to the throne of Osiris for the ritual of the Weighing of the Heart. He was also the patron of embalmers. Anubis had several epithets including 'foremost of the westerners' (i.e the dead buried on the west bank of the Nile); 'he who is upon his mountain' (i.e the desert cliffs overlooking the

cemeteries); 'Lord of the Sacred land' (i.e the desert in which the burials were located); 'the one presiding over the god's pavillion' (i.e the place where embalming took place, or the burial chamber); and 'he who is in the place of embalming'.

Anubis was depicted as a jackal or as a man with the head of a jackal. Priests who prepared bodies for burial and conducted burial ceremonies are thought to have impersonated the god by wearing jackal masks. Since jackals were common scavengers in Egyptian burial sites, the honouring of Anubis in this guise may have represented a way of protecting the dead from molestation.

Astarte

This goddess appears to have been almost interchangeable with Anat. She was also associated with war (particularly with horses and chariots), and was thought to protect the king in battle. She was of Syrian origin, and there is no evidence for her cult in Egypt before the Eighteenth Dynasty (c.1150–c.1295 BC).

She was usually represented as a naked woman riding a horse and wearing the *atef*-crown or bull's horns on her head. She was variously regarded as the daughter of Re or of Ptah, and was thought to be one of Seth's consorts.

Atum

Atum ('the All') was the self-engendered creator god who arose from the primordial waters of chaos, Nun, in order to form the primeval mound and to bring the elements of the cosmos into being. As the head of the so-called Ennead (or nine gods), he held the title 'Lord to the Limits of the Sky'. His cult

▲ *As a funerary deity, Atum's presence is significant on the walls of non-royal Theban tombs of the New Kingdom (c.1550–c.1069 BC) such as that of Sennedjem. c.1300 BC.*

centre was at Heliopolis, and he was regarded very much as a solar deity (at some stage he was syncretized with the pre-eminent sun god, Re, in order to form the combined deity Re-Atum).

Atum was very much associated with kingship, and was believed to lift the dead king from his pyramid to the stars. Later, as a result of the gradual democratization of funerary religion, he came to be regarded as the

▶ *Relative size is used to denote importance in Egyptian art, as shown by this diorite statue of Horemheb kneeling before the seated figure of Atum. c.1300 BC.*

protector not only of the king but of all dead people on their way into the Afterlife.

Atum was usually represented as a man wearing the Double Crown of Upper and Lower Egypt, although he could also be portrayed as a snake. Additional animals were deemed sacred to him, including the lion, bull, mongoose, lizard and dung beetle.

Baba

At his most dangerous, Baba was believed to murder humans and feed on their entrails. He was associated with aggression and virility – especially those of the king. Sometimes his penis was said to be the bolt on the doors of heaven, and at other times it was the mast on the ferry in the Netherworld. He was believed to be able to ward off snakes and to control darkness and turbulent waters. He was represented as a baboon.

Eye of Re

According to this strange concept, the eye of the sun god was in fact separate from him and could act independently. In the myth of *The Destruction of Humankind* it manifested itself first as Hathór and then as the more ferocious divine female force, Sekhmet.

The Eye was also identified with the cobra goddess Wadjet, one of the protective female deities of kingship, who appears rearing up at the front of the royal headdress, ready to spit poison at the king's enemies. This rearing snake is known as the uraeus.

Geb

As the divine personification of the earth, Geb was a god of fertility. For this reason, he was sometimes coloured green and was visualized with plants growing out of him. He was often depicted reclining beneath the arched body of

◄ The influence of the Near Eastern goddess Astarte was widespread in the ancient world. This pectoral plaque depicting the goddess was found in the Camirus cemetery on Rhodes. Early Greek.

◄ The sistrum was shaken like a rattle by priestesses of Hathor. Late Period.

his sister-consort, the sky goddess Nut. In *The Creation Myth of Heliopolis*, Geb and Nut were the two children of Shu and Tefnut. They were lovers, but were forcibly separated by their father Shu, the god of air.

Geb was always represented in human form, sometimes with an erect penis. He occasionally wore the Red Crown of Lower Egypt, but more often had a white-fronted goose on his head. Thus, his daughter Isis could be described as the 'Egg of the Goose'. Like his father Shu, he had a dark side to him, which was expressed in funerary religion: he was considered able to trap the dead in his body. Earthquakes were described as the 'laughter of Geb'.

Hathor

A mother goddess, Hathor was associated with love, fertility, sexuality, music, dance and alcohol. She was sometimes represented entirely anthropomorphically, in the form of a cow, or as a woman with cow's ears. When in human form, her headdress could be one of cow's horns with a solar disc, or a falcon on a perch. She was also a sky goddess, and was regarded as a vast cow who straddled the heavens, with her four legs marking the four cardinal points.

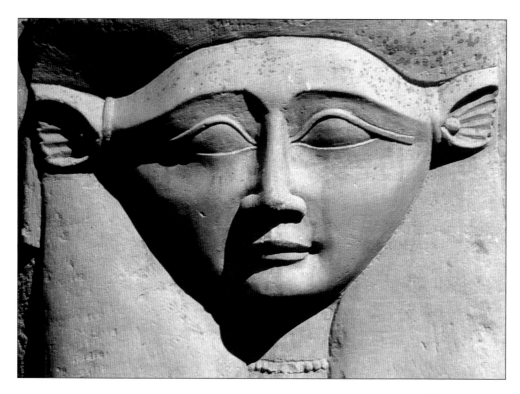

◄ The cow-goddess Hathor was often depicted with a human face but with cow's ears on column capitals, such as this one at Dendera, site of the most famous of her temples. Hathor's representation as a cow identified her as the great mother, symbolizing fertility, motherhood and nurture.

▼ The favourable support and protection bestowed on the king by the whole of the divine world is epitomized by the image of the cow goddess Hathor suckling the adult ruler (in this case Amenhotep II). 18th Dynasty.

In various contexts she was honoured as 'Lady of the West' or 'Lady of the Western Mountain', 'Lady of Byblos', 'Lady of Turquoise' and 'Lady of Faience'. The 'west' or 'western mountain' refers to the place of the setting sun and thus, by analogy, the realm of the dead. Byblos was a port on the Lebanese coast, important for Egyptian trade and particularly in the importing of cedar wood, since Egypt had no native timber for the construction of boats or large buildings. Egypt exploited turquoise mines from Predynastic times, especially in the Sinai Peninsula (a temple to Hathor has been found at the mining site of Serabit el-Khadim). Faience was a much-used glazed ceramic material composed primarily of crushed quartz or quartz sand, and usually a blue or green colour (perhaps a cheap imitation of turquoise).

Like Isis, Hathor was considered to be the mother of the falcon deity Horus, and thus of the king (who was closely identified with Horus). Her name means 'the House of Horus'. However, inscriptions on the temple of Horus at Edfu refer to Hathor marrying this deity. The king was sometimes depicted being suckled by the goddess in cow form, as shown by a wonderful statue in the Cairo Museum from Deir el-Bahri of the Eighteenth-Dynasty pharaoh Amenhotep II (c.1427– c.1400 BC) enjoying just such sustenance. Although she was sometimes identified with the Eye of Re, she appeared on other occasions as the sun god's daughter.

From the Old Kingdom (c.2686– c.2181 BC) Hathor's chief cult centre was at Dendera. Her festivities appear to have been suitably debauched. An emblem of her cult was the sistrum (or rattle), which would have been shaken as part of the ritual proceedings. The existing temple on this site dates to the Graeco-Roman Period, and is dedicated to the triad Hathor, Horus and Ihy, Hathor's son, who played the sistrum in her honour.

Horus

The king of Egypt was closely identified with Horus from the beginning of Dynastic history (c.3100 BC). The god was represented as a falcon, or with the head of a falcon, and one of his most ubiquitous symbols was the 'Eye of Horus' (the *udjat-* or *wadjat*-eye). In one version of the myth of *The Contendings of Horus and Seth*, Horus had both his eyes gouged out. In other versions he lost (and then regained) only his left eye. As the weaker of the two, it came to be associated with the moon while the right eye was associated with the sun. Because in both instances his eyesight was eventually cured, his eye came to symbolize healing (*udjat* literally means 'sound'). It was used as a

◄ *As the god of kingship, Horus was often shown wearing the combined Red and White Crowns of Lower and Upper Egypt, as on this column at the temple of Kom Ombo.*

▲ *The 'Eye of Horus' is a ubiquitous emblem in ancient Egyptian art. It symbolized healing, wholeness, strength and perfection. New Kingdom.*

protective amulet, symbolizing strength and perfection, and also represented the waxing and waning moon.

Horus's name means 'He Who is Above', and is probably linked to his status as a god of the sky and to the high soaring of the falcon. As 'Horus in the Horizon' he was called a Horemakhet and in this capacity he was amalgamated with the solar deity Re to become Re-Horakhty.

From the Late Period (c.747 BC) he appeared in his child form, Hor-pa-khered (whom the Greeks called Harpocrates) on a form of stela known as a *cippus* of Horus. He was usually depicted treading crocodiles underfoot and grasping snakes, scorpions and other such dangerous creatures. It is always clear that he was intended to be a child because he was pictured naked, sporting a particular hairstyle known as the 'side-lock of youth'. The idea behind

this aspect of the god was that since Horus as a young boy had managed to survive certain dangers, a ritual could be performed using his image to protect children from similar threats (or perhaps to cure snake bites and scorpion stings). Water was poured over the *cippi* (which were covered in spells), causing the liquid to be imbued with their magical potency, so it could be ritually imbibed or applied.

Horus was honoured as an element of the divine triad at the cult centre of Abydos, but he is most associated with the temple at Edfu (ancient Mesen), where he was worshipped as part of a triad with his consort Hathor and their child Harsomtus. He was also closely associated with Hierakonpolis ('Town of the Hawk', ancient Nekhen) in the south and a town called Behdet in the Delta. As 'Horus of Behdet' he was represented as a winged sun disc.

▲ *On the back of one of Tutankhamun's thrones, the god Heh kneels on the hieroglyphic sign for gold, and clutches notched palm branches, symbolizing the passing of time. 18th Dynasty.*

▼ *Khepri is depicted here in the tomb of Seti I on a boat on the waters of Nun. The wish is expressed in the early royal funerary texts that the sun should come into being in its name of Khepri. 19th Dynasty.*

Huh/Heh

The frog-headed god Huh was the personification of formlessness and infinity. His consort was the snake-headed goddess Hauhet. He was often represented anthropomorphically holding in each hand a palm-rib (the hieroglyph for 'year').

Isis

Like Hathor, Isis was a mother goddess and was identified more specifically as the mother of Horus, and thus of the king. The image of her suckling Horus (especially found in the form of numerous bronze figurines dating to the Late and Graeco-Roman Periods) is reminiscent of the Christian mother-and-child icon.

Isis tended to be represented as a woman with a throne, or solar disc between cow's horns, on her head. She was sometimes regarded as the personification of the throne: the hieroglyph for her name is the image of a throne, and her lap came to be seen as the throne of Egypt. She was also frequently depicted with huge, sheltering wings. She was part of the Ennead of Heliopolis, and as consort to Osiris and mother of Horus, she appeared in the triad of deities worshipped at Abydos. Her best-known cult centre was on the island of Philae, on the southern border of Egypt, near Aswan. She was particularly closely associated with magic. Her ability to heal and to transform herself into any guise she desired are evident in the myths about her. Two important manifestations of this goddess were the 'Great White Sow of Heliopolis' and the Isis-cow which gave birth to the sacred Apis Bull of Memphis. Her following eventually spread beyond Egypt, to Syria, Palestine, Greece and throughout the whole Roman Empire, and she was worshipped until well into Christian times.

▶ *Several species of dung beetle are found in Egypt, but the large sacred scarab, Scarabeus sacer, is the one most commonly represented in ancient Egyptian art.*

Khepri

The god Khepri (which literally means 'He who is Coming into Being') was a creator and solar deity. He was represented as a scarab or dung beetle, or as a beetle-headed man. The choice of a dung beetle to portray a creator god and the manifestation of the rising sun is significant because of the activities of such a beetle. It was observed to roll its eggs in a ball of dung along the ground, and the ball was identified with the sun. The baby beetles were seen to emerge from the dung, as if life was emerging from the primeval mound, and so dung beetles were thought capable of spontaneous creation.

From the Middle Kingdom (c.2055–c.1650 BC) onwards the scarab-form amulet was very popular, and was worn in bracelets and necklaces. Scarabs were used as funerary talismans, and were placed over the heart of the deceased to keep it from confessing sins during its interrogation.

Khnum

Khnum was an ancient deity represented as a man with the head of a ram, or in entirely ram form. The type of ram used to portray him was the earliest one to be domesticated in Egypt – the *Ovis longipes* – which had curly horns extending horizontally from the head. The ancient Egyptian for 'ram' was *ba*, which was also the word for a concept akin to our 'personality' (possibly those non-physical attributes which make any one human being unique, or perhaps the moral essence of a person's motivation and movement). It may well then have been thanks to the ancient Egyptian love of puns that Khnum came to be

regarded as the *ba* of the sun god Re, and so this deity was represented with a ram's head while passing through the Netherworld in his solar barque. Certainly the *ba* of the dead appeared to be more mobile than their *ka* ('spirit').

Connected with Khnum's capacity as a creator god was his role as patron deity

of potters, and his association with the fertile soil, the annual inundation and the Nile cataracts. His chief cult centre was situated on the island of Elephantine, at the first cataract at the southern border of Egypt. Another important temple to Khnum was located at Esna. Here his consort was the lioness-goddess Menhyt. And it was here that the Festival of the Potter's Wheel was celebrated each year.

▼ *The ram was a symbol of fertility and male virility. It was used to represent the creator god Khnum, who fashioned the universe out of clay.*

◄ *Khonsu was depicted as a young man usually wrapped in the bandages of a mummy or other tight-fitting garment and carrying the royal crook, flail and sceptre.*

Khonsu

The son of Amun and Mut, Khonsu's name means 'wanderer', which probably refers to the passage of the moon across the sky, as he was a lunar deity. In the late period, he was also considered an important god of healing. His chief cult centre was at Thebes.

Kuk

The frog-headed god Kuk was the personification of darkness. His consort was the snake-headed Kauket.

Min

As a god of fertility, Min was represented in semi-mummified human form, his left hand holding his erect phallus and his right arm raised. The key feature of his headdress was two tall plumes. The emblems of his cult were the lettuce and an unidentified shape which could possibly be a door-bolt, a barbed arrow, a lightning bolt or a pair of fossil shells. He was a particularly

► *Ramesses I is depicted on the wall of his tomb face to face with Nefertem, the divine personification of the lotus blossom.*

ancient deity, and was also regarded as a protector of the mining regions in the Eastern Desert.

His main cult centres were at Koptos and Akhmim (which the Greeks called Panopolis because they identified their god Pan with Min). He was sometimes described as the son of Isis, but on other occasions he was said to be her consort, with Horus as their son. By the New Kingdom (c.1550–c.1069 BC) he had merged with the Theban deity Amun.

Nefertem

This deity was associated with the lotus blossom, and was represented in male human form with the blue lotus (*Nymphaea caerulea*) on his head (see *Plants and Flowers in Mythology*). His headdress sometimes also incorporated two plumes and two necklace counterpoises.

The *Creation Myth of Hermopolis Magna* states that the sun rose from the primeval lotus flower, and Nefertem was with her consort Seth and their child Sobek, the crocodile god. As a mother goddess she was given the epithet 'Great Cow' (as were the goddesses Nut and Hathor). She was also considered a creator goddess and as such was equated with the primordial waters of chaos, Nun.

Together with Isis, Nephthys and the scorpion goddess, Selket, she was a funerary goddess: they each protected one of the 'Four Sons of Horus' who in turn looked after the internal organs of the deceased. Neith was specifically associated with the jackal-headed Duamutef who protected the stomach and upper intestines. She was also linked with the linen mummy bandages because she was believed to have invented weaving.

Nephthys

In later mythology, Nephthys was regarded as the mother of the jackal-headed god of embalming, Anubis, as a result of a union with Osiris. She was the sister of Isis, Osiris and Seth (of whom she was also thought to be a consort). She appears to have been an aide to her better-known sister Isis. Like her, Nephthys was usually depicted in human form, but could also be represented as a kite. Her name means 'Lady of the Mansion', and her headdress consisted of the hieroglyphs for this epithet (a basket on top of the enclosure wall of a grand house).

Nephthys was associated with the head of the deceased or the coffin (in collaboration with Isis at the foot). She was also one of the protective canopic deities: she protected the baboon-headed son of Horus, Hapy, who in turn guarded the lungs of the deceased.

closely linked with the sun god. The Pyramid Texts of the Old Kingdom refer to Nefertem as 'the lotus blossom which is before the nose of Re' (Utterance 266). His universal importance is expressed in his title 'Protector of the Two Lands' (*khener tawy*), referring to Upper and Lower Egypt.

Nefertem was worshipped at Memphis as the son of god Ptah and the lioness-goddess Sekhmet, so he was sometimes depicted as lion-headed. He was also occasionally referred to as the son of the cat-goddess Bastet or, to complicate matters further, as the son of the cobra-goddess Wadjet at Buto.

Neith

A particularly ancient goddess whose main cult centre was at Sais in the Delta, Neith rose to particular prominence during the Twenty-sixth Dynasty (664–525 BC), when Sais was the home of the ruling family and the capital of Egypt. Her emblem was a shield with crossed arrows, emphasizing her association with warfare (the Greeks later identified her with their goddess Athena). This symbol has been found on objects dating all the way back to the First Dynasty (c.3100–c.2890 BC). She is usually depicted wearing the Red Crown of Lower Egypt. Neith formed a triad

▲ *In the Pyramid Texts of the Old Kingdom (c.2686–c.2181 BC), the sky goddess Nut, painted inside this coffin of Seti I, is variously described as the king's coffin, sarcophagus and tomb. 19th Dynasty.*

▼ *In illustrations of the Heliopolitan creation myth, as here on the papyrus of Nespakashuty, Nut arches naked over her consort Geb, the earth god.*

Nun

The god Nun was the divine personification of the primordial waters of chaos, which preceded creation. He was described as the 'eldest father' and 'maker of humankind'. It was believed that after creation had taken place, chaos was continued to exist beyond the edges of the universe, and in the Netherworld, and was the place of social outcasts and demons.

The mudbrick enclosure walls of temples were sometimes constructed in curved courses (pan bedding), which resulted in a wavy effect. This was possibly meant to imitate the waters of Nun, the temple itself symbolizing the universe. Nun was also thought to be present within the context of the temple, in the form of the sacred lake.

Nun could be represented as a baboon, or with a frog's head, or in an entirely human form, with a beard. In the latter guise he was often depicted holding the solar barque aloft. His consort was the snake-headed goddess Naunet.

Nut

The goddess Nut was the divine personification of the sky. According to the Heliopolitan creation myth, she was one of the children of Shu and Tefnut, and the sister and consort of Geb, the earth god. The darkness at night was explained by the belief that Nut swallowed the sun in the evening and gave birth to it at dawn, so it spent the night hours travelling through her body. This image was often depicted on the ceilings of tombs and on the undersides of sarcophagus lids, expressing the belief that Nut divinely personified the

▼ *Ani's Book of the Dead shows the dead man being led by Horus to the enthroned Osiris, who is attended by his sisters Isis and Nephthys.*

▶ *In the papyrus Book of the Dead of the priest of Amun-Re, Chensumose, the djed-pillar, considered to be the embodiment of Osiris's backbone, is semi-personified: ankhs hang from its arms and it holds aloft an encircled snake. 21st Dynasty.*

coffin and burial chamber. Because the sun was said to be born from her each morning, the deceased might be reborn from her into the Afterlife.

She was usually shown as a woman arching over the earth, but could also be represented as a cow. The 'Divine Cow' was believed to carry Re, the sun god, on her back each morning.

Osiris

God of the dead and the Afterlife (as well as of rebirth and fertility), Osiris was represented in a mummified anthropomorphic form, often holding a crook and flail, and with the *atef*-crown (described as 'sky piercing') on his

head. His skin could be green or black (signifying fertility or the thick black Nile silt), or white (the colour of the linen mummy bandages). One of his emblems was the *djed*-pillar, a symbol of stability, which was equated with his backbone and was particularly revered at his cult centre of Busiris (ancient Djedu)

in the Delta.

The chief cult centre of Osiris was his legendary burial place (and consequently an important pilgrims' destination) Abydos (ancient Abdjw), where he was worshipped together with his sister-consort Isis and their son Horus, and where an annual festival was held in his honour. He was a member of the important Ennead (nine gods) of Heliopolis (see *Creation Myths*), a genealogy that appears for the first time in the Pyramid Texts of the Fifth Dynasty. These were found – as the name implies – on the interior walls of certain pyramids.

Epithets applied to Osiris included 'eternally good' and 'foremost of the westerners' (that is the dead, who were thought, like the sun, to enter the Netherworld in the west). He was assimilated

▲ *The Theban tomb-builders' village of Deir el-Medina, located in the desert about 2km (1 mile) west of the Nile Valley, consists of about 70 limestone and mudbrick houses of uniform size.*

with two Memphite deities, the creator god Ptah, and the hawk-headed funerary deity Sokar, forming the syncretized funerary god Ptah-Sokar-Osiris.

The deceased king of Egypt was identified with Osiris from at least the Fifth Dynasty (c.2494–c.2345 BC). By about 2000 BC, a democratization of funerary religion had begun to take place, and dead people other than the king were also identified with Osiris.

Ptah

Recognized as the chief deity of the city of Memphis, Ptah was worshipped as part of a triad with his consort the lioness-goddess Sekhmet and the lotus-god Nefertem. At a later stage, Imhotep, the deified architect of Djoser's Step Pyramid Complex at Saqqara, was regarded as a son of Ptah (see

◄ *Wooden figures of Ptah-Sokar-Osiris were part of a wealthy Egyptian's funerary equipment. Miniature rolls of papyrus might be deposited in a compartment in the base. Late Period.*

Deification of Mortals). As chief creator god, Ptah was regarded as the patron deity of craftsmen, and so was an important figure at Deir el-Medina, the village of craftsmen who were responsible for the tombs in the Valley of the Kings. At Memphis, the High Priest of his cult held the title 'Great Over-seer of Craftsmen' (*wer kherep hemw*).

Ptah was represented in human, semi-mummified form, wearing a skullcap and holding a staff which combined the *was*-sceptre of power, the *djed*-pillar of stability and the *ankh*-sign for life. From the Middle Kingdom (c.2055–c.1650 BC) onwards he was depicted with a straight beard.

During the Old Kingdom (c.2686–c.2181 BC) Ptah was merged with the Memphite hawk-headed funerary deity Sokar, creating the god Ptah-Sokar. This composite deity went on to become Ptah-Sokar-Osiris in the Late Period. Wooden, mummiform, hawk-headed figures of this god were often placed in tombs as part of the funerary equipment.

Re

With good reason, the ancient Egyptians considered the sun to be a potent life force; together with the annual inundation of the Nile, it was responsible for their successful harvests. Re was the pre-eminent solar deity.

His cult centre was at Heliopolis (called Iunu by the ancient Egyptians and now a suburb of modern Cairo) where an extremely powerful priesthood officiated. From the Fourth-Dynasty reign of Djedefre (c.2566–c.2558 BC) onwards, one of the king's five names was introduced with the epithet 'Son of Re', emphasizing the association of the king with the god. The focal point of Re's cult was the obelisk, or *benben* stone (deriving from the verb *weben,* 'to shine forth').

In the myth of the Destruction of Humankind, Re is described as having the bones, flesh and hair of an old man, but his divinity is evident because they are of silver, gold and lapis lazuli (the last was considered especially valuable by the ancient Egyptians because it had to be imported from as far away as Badakhshan in north-eastern Afghanistan). This description may be that of a cult statue, such as would be found in the *naos* or shrine of each temple, housing the very essence or potency of the deity in question. The myth also states that he was self-created, coming into being in Nun, the primordial waters.

Re was frequently represented anthropomorphically, but with the head of a ram or a hawk wearing a sun-disc headdress. As the sun god, he was thought to voyage across the sky in a boat during the twelve hours of daylight, and through the Netherworld during the hours of darkness. In another version of the myth of his nightly journey, he was swallowed by Nut, the sky goddess, and

▼ *The royal title 'Son of Re' is written with the hieroglyphic signs of a duck (meaning 'son') and a solar disc. Karnak.*

travelled through her body to be reborn each morning.

The sun god was ubiquitous and powerful. By the process of syncretism, Re was amalgamated with other deities such as Amun, becoming Amun-Re, and Horus, becoming Re-Horakhty ('Horus of the Two Horizons'). Or he might be identified with other gods; one of the texts inscribed on the walls of some tombs in the Valley of the Kings during the New Kingdom (c.1550–c.1069 BC) is the 'Litany of Re', in which Re is identified with Osiris, god of the dead.

Sekhmet

The goddess Sekhmet was the ferocious aspect of female divinity, whether of Hathor, Bastet (the cat goddess of Bubastis in the Delta) or the mother goddess Mut whose temple at Karnak was filled with statues of Sekhmet by the Eighteenth-Dynasty king Amenhotep III (c.1390–1352 BC): it is thought that there was one for each day of the year. She was associated with war and battle, and helped the king to vanquish his enemies. Her name literally means 'the Powerful One', and she was visualized, appropriately, as a lioness, or at least as a woman with the head of a lioness. She wore a sun disc identifying her as the daughter of Re.

Sekhmet played an important role in the capital city of Memphis, as the consort of the creator god Ptah and the mother of Nefertem.

Seth

Seth was Osiris's 'wicked' brother and, as such, was a member of the Heliopolitan family of gods and goddesses. He was associated with chaos, infertility and the desert, but in certain geographical areas (such as the north-eastern Delta) and at certain times in Egyptian history, he was highly honoured. There were kings of the Nineteenth and Twentieth Dynasties, for example, whose names derived from his, such as Seti and Sethnakhte. His worship recognized that chaos had to be acknowledged before order could be seen to exist, and though the desert was an arid and dangerous place it was also of enormous value to the Egyptians (particularly for its natural resources such as gold, amethyst and turquoise). The god had an important cult centre at Naqada in Upper Egypt. Tradition maintained this had been the place of his violent birth from the sky goddess Nut.

Seth was represented in the form of an animal that cannot be conclusively identified: it had a long curved snout, pricked, flat-topped ears, a canine body and a forked tail. He was sometimes shown as a man with this animal's head. It is possible that this animal may have

▲ *The bizarre Seth animal, with its long snout and pricked, blunt-ended ears, often appeared on magical objects, such as wands designed to protect against harm.*

belonged to a species that is now extinct, but it is more likely to have been fabricated to produce a disconcerting appearance for a deity associated with trouble and barrenness. Seth could also be represented as a pig, a donkey or a hippopotamus (see *The Contendings of Horus and Seth*).

Shu

The divine personification of air as well as sunlight, Shu's name probably means 'He who Rises Up'. Although he was thought to bring the sun to life each morning and to protect it against the serpent demon Apophis in the Netherworld, he was also often associated with the lunar deities Thoth and Khonsu. Perhaps improbably, he was additionally thought to be the leader of a pack of demons that threatened to torture the deceased.

He was represented in human form with a feather on his head, and was often depicted standing between his offspring, Geb (the earth god) and Nut (the sky goddess), supporting the latter. He could also be visualized with the head of a lion, and it was in this guise that he was referred to as an 'Eye of Re', and was worshipped at Leontopolis (Tell el-Muqdam) in the Delta.

Sobek

The crocodile god was represented either as the reptile itself or as a man with the head of a crocodile. Sobek was worshipped in the Faiyum and at the temple of Kom Ombo. Sobek was associated with the might of the Pharaoh, and in the form of Sobek-Re he was worshipped as a manifestation of the Solar diety. His consort was Hathor and Khonsu, elsewhere said to be the son of Amun and Mut, was regarded as their child.

▲ *Incorporated into the design of this ivory headrest found in the tomb of Tutankhamun is Shu, the god of air, who here supports the head of the sleeper rather than his usual load, his daughter Nut, the sky goddess.*

▼ *The ancient Egyptians worshipped Sobek in the form of a crocodile, or with the head of a crocodile, in the hope that this would help to protect them from the hidden dangers of the River Nile. Kom Ombo.*

Sokar

This god was associated with the earth and fertility, but particularly with death and the cemetery of the capital city of Memphis. His funerary association led him to be syncretized with Osiris, and his Memphite importance resulted in his syncretism with the chief deity there, Ptah – hence the invention of the god Ptah-Sokar-Osiris. Sokar's association with Ptah also meant they shared the same consort, the lioness goddess Sekhmet.

▶ *In his role as scribe and messenger of the gods, Thoth was usually represented as a man with the head of an ibis. 19th Dynasty. Valley of the Kings.*

▼ *One of two colossal granite statues of Thoth, the god of wisdom and writing, represented as a baboon. They are all that remains of the once great temple at Hermopolis Magna. 18th Dynasty.*

In the Pyramid Texts, Sokar is described as the maker of 'royal bones'. He was represented as a mummified man, sometimes with the head of a hawk. Wooden statuettes of him were placed in tombs together with a host of other funerary equipment. He could also be portrayed as a mound of earth surmounted by a boat containing the head of a hawk.

Sokar's chief cult centre was at Memphis. During the festival held there in his honour, his devotees wore strings of onions around their necks. Onions were certainly used in the embalming process – their skins or whole bulbs were placed over the eyes or stuffed into the ears or the body cavity. Today onion is used to disguise nasty smells, and in folklore it is believed to combat infection.

Tefnut

As one of the cosmic deities of the Ennead, Tefnut was the divine personification of moisture. To tie in with the imagery of symmetrical pairs, when her brother-consort Shu was associated with sunlight, Tefnut was associated with the moon.

Like Shu, Tefnut could be regarded as an 'Eye of Re', and as such was represented with a lioness head (and was worshipped at Leontopolis). She also appeared in the form of a rearing cobra, in which case she was identified with the *uraeus* on the front of the royal headdress. When depicted in human form, she wore a sun disc encircled by a cobra on her head.

Thoth

The god of wisdom and the scribal profession, Thoth manifested himself as a baboon, an ibis or a man with the head of an ibis. He was frequently represented recording important proceedings, such as at the 'Weighing of the Heart' ceremony which was believed to take place after death. He was also closely associated with the moon, so was often depicted wearing a lunar disc and crescent on his head.

His chief cult centre was that of Hermopolis Magna (ancient Khmun; modern el-Ashmunein) in Middle Egypt, where all that remains today are two huge statues of baboons erected by the Eighteenth-Dynasty king Amenhotep III (c.1390–c.1352 BC). These statues are extremely impressive; they are sculpted from great blocks of quartzite, are about 4.5m (15ft) tall (excluding the bases), and weigh about 35 tons each.

During the Ptolemaic Period (332–30 BC) Thoth was identified with the Greek god Hermes; for this reason the city of Khmun became known as Hermopolis ('the city of Hermes').

Wadjet

The ancient goddess Wadjet was nearly always portrayed in the form of a cobra wearing the Red Crown of Lower Egypt. The Egyptians regarded the cobra as a symbol of sovereignty. Wadjet had her cult centre at Buto in the Delta. Her name means 'the Green One' or 'She of the Papyrus'. Together with the vulture goddess Nekhbet (whose cult was based at El-Kab in Upper Egypt) she was believed to protect the king. One of the ruler's five names was his *nebty* or 'two ladies' name, referring to these two particular goddesses. Wadjet appeared as the *uraeus* ('she who rears up') on the king's forehead, poised to spit venom at an unsuspecting enemy. She was also sometimes represented as a lioness. ◆

▲ *The vulture head and cobra on the brow of Tutankhamun's solid-gold mummy mask are decorated with glass and faience, with quartz, carnelian, lapis lazuli and obsidian inlay. The uraeus, or rearing snake, was poised to protect the king from attack by his enemies.*

▼ *The Eye of Horus, flanked by Nekhbet, the vulture goddess of Upper Egypt, and Wadjet, the cobra goddess of Lower Egypt, adorns this pectoral pendant found wrapped under the twelfth layer of linen bandages on Tutankhamun's mummy.*

Myths
and their
Settings

S tories or myths evolved in all
cultures in order to provide a
divine explanation for the
fundamentals of human existence. In
ancient Egypt the realm of the gods
was clearly envisaged to reflect that
of mortals, as a means of bringing
the divine world to life and
furnishing the gods and goddesses
with a certain accessibility.

Surprisingly few myths actually
survive considering the vast time-
span of the Egyptian culture and the
huge number of its deities, as well as
the cult centres with accompanying
priesthoods that might have been
expected to generate such literature.
It is likely that there was a strong
oral tradition and that many stories
have been lost, but those to which we
do still have access were inscribed in
hieroglyphs on the walls of temples
and tombs, or written on papyrus in
the more cursive hieratic and
demotic scripts.

The myths that follow have been
selected to show how the Egyptians
assimilated the mysteries of creation,
life and death into their world-view,
and to illustrate the recognizably
human characters of the major
deities, their displays of emotion and
the relationships between them. Each
myth is accompanied by explanatory
details which help to set it in a
historical and sociological context.

◀ *The creation myth of Heliopolis envisaged the*
sky and earth as anthropomorphic deities: Nut
the sky goddess and Geb the god of the earth.

Creation Myths

Several explanations as to how the universe came into being survive from ancient Egypt. Each major centre of religious belief had its own version of the myth of creation, with a different main creator deity who was self-engendered and who went on to generate the other gods and goddesses before creating humankind. The particular deities mentioned in each of the stories relate to the geographical areas where the myths originated. It is impossible to say which of the myths was the most widely accepted at any one time.

The Creation Myth of Memphis

Ptah was the self-engendered creator god who was referred to as the 'father of the gods from whom all life emerged'. He brought the universe into being by conceiving all aspects of it in his heart, then speaking his thoughts out loud. First he created the other deities, and then towns with shrines in which to house them. He provided wood, clay and stone statues to act as bodies for the spirits or divine power (*ka*) of the deities, and offerings to be made to them forever. All things, including all people and animals, were brought into being by Ptah declaring their names.

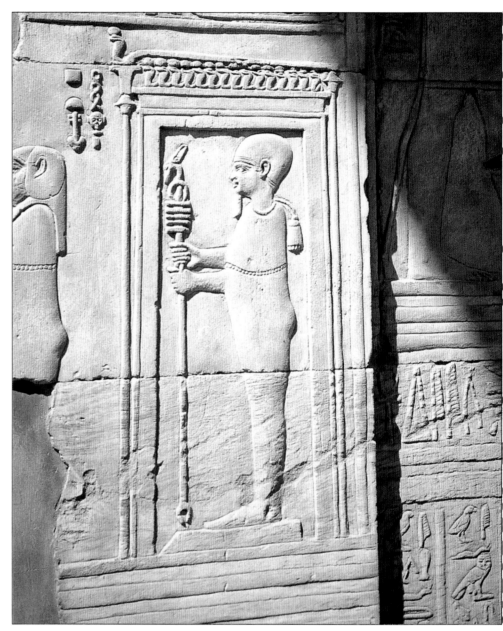

▲ *Ptah's role as a creator god made him the ideal candidate for patron deity of craftsmen. His high priest was given the title of 'Lord of the Master Craftsmen'. Kom Ombo.*

The Creation Myth of Elephantine

The creator god of this cult centre was the ram-headed deity of the southern cataract region, Khnum. He created the universe by modelling the other gods, as well as humankind (both Egyptians and all those who spoke other languages), animals, birds, fish, reptiles and plants out of clay on his potter's wheel. He paid particular attention to the moulding of the human body, getting the blood to flow over the bones and stretching the skin carefully over the body. He took special care with the installation of the respiratory and digestive systems, the vertebrae, and the reproductive organs. Afterwards, he ensured the continuation of the human race by watching over conception and labour.

The Creation Myth of Hermopolis Magna

This myth begins by concentrating on the elements that were necessary for creation to take place. The fundamental factors were arranged in four male-female pairs: primordial water (Nun and Naunet); air or hidden power (Amun and Amaunet); darkness (Kuk and Kauket); and formlessness or infinity, otherwise interpreted as flood force (Huh and Hauhet). These divine personifications

▼ This papyrus scene, from the Third Intermediate Period Book of the Dead of Tameniu, shows the sky goddess Nut arching over her prostrate consort, the earth deity Geb. The fertility of the earth is clearly indicated, and as was usual, the cosmological deities are represented in entirely human form.

◄ Thoth had several guises, including that of a man with the head of an ibis, as shown here in a wooden figure with a bronze head dating to the Late Period.

of the basic elements of the cosmos are referred to as the Ogdoad (Greek for 'group of eight'; in Egyptian, *khmun*). The four male gods were all frog-headed, and the four goddesses were snake-headed. At some point the eight elements interacted to create a burst of energy, allowing creation to take place.

There are two versions of the events that followed in this creation myth. In one version a primeval mound of earth described as the Isle of Flame rose up out of the primordial water. The god Thoth, in the form of an ibis, placed a cosmic egg on the mound of earth. The egg cracked, hatching the sun, which immediately rose up into the sky.

According to the alternative version, a lotus flower (divinely personified as the deity Nefertem) was bobbing on the surface of the primordial waters when the petals opened and the sun rose out of it. On this occasion the sun was identified as Horus.

The Creation Myth of Heliopolis

Before anything existed or creation had taken place, there was darkness and endless, lifeless water, divinely personified as Nun. A mound of fertile silt emerged from this watery chaos. The self-engendered solar creator god Atum ('the All' or 'the Complete One') appeared upon the mound. By masturbating (or sneezing, according to other versions of the myth) he was able to spit out the deities Shu (the divine personification of air) and Tefnut (moisture). Now that a male-female pair existed, they were able to procreate more conventionally. The results of their sexual union were Geb (the earth) and Nut (the sky). These two were forcibly separated by their father Shu, who lifted Nut up to her place above the earth.

The so-called Ennead (Greek for 'group of nine'; in Egyptian *pesedjet*) of Heliopolis includes these deities: Atum ('the Bull of the Ennead'), Shu, Tefnut, Geb and Nut, and is completed by the offspring of the latter two gods – Osiris, Isis, Seth and Nephthys.   ◆

The Creation Myths in Context

The principle underlying all the different creation myths is that of order being established out of chaos. A state of primordial wateriness is used to represent chaos, out of which emerges a mound, and on it a solar deity. This mythological chain of events clearly reflects the annual flooding of the Nile and the subsiding of the water to reveal deposits of thick black silt, which were incredibly fertile but which required the sun for growth to take place.

All the explanations tend to hinge on the fertility of the land (thanks to the Nile inundation) and the heat of the sun. However, at Memphis the priests devised a myth centred around their supreme deity Ptah, which was decidedly less earthy and rather more metaphysical. Instead of relying on solar energy for creation to take place, the Memphite explanation depended upon the harnessing of three abstract catalysts: *heka* (magic or divine energy), *sia* (divine knowledge) and *hu* (divine utterance). This is similar to the 'logos' doctrine of the biblical New Testament, according to which the word of God became incarnate in the body of Jesus, the second person of the trinity.

The Background to the Creation Myth of Memphis

Memphis (ancient Men-nefer) is about 24km (15 miles) south of modern Cairo in the area of the modern village of Mit Rahina. It was founded as the administrative capital of Egypt at the beginning of the First Dynasty (c.3100 BC), but very little of this ancient capital survives today, mainly because its ruins were quarried during the medieval period for stone to use in the building of Cairo's churches and mosques.

The Memphis creation myth has survived inscribed on a rectangular slab of black granite measuring 92 x 137cm

▲ *The Shabaqo Stone bears a hieroglyphic inscription which is partially obscured by the slab's subsequent use as a mill stone.*

▼ *From the Middle Kingdom Period, the god Ptah was portrayed wearing a strap-on beard like that of the living king.*

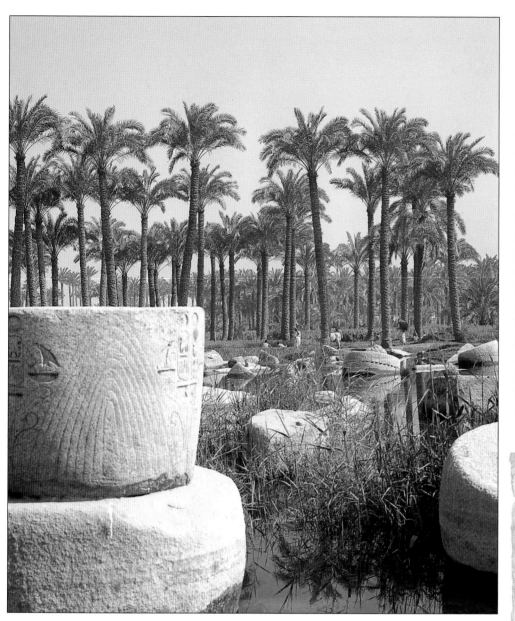

◀ *The water table is so high in the region of Memphis that the ancient administrative capital is all but submerged. Preservation of this great city is extremely poor.*

During the embalming process the brain was removed through the nose and discarded as if a waste product, while the heart was always left safely inside the body. The belief was that the dead person required his or her body and – even more importantly – heart in order to be reborn into the Afterlife. The dead person was judged by weighing his or her heart in a balance against the feather of Maat, the goddess of truth.

Order and chaos

The Egyptians had a high regard for order, as is evident from their carefully regulated social structure and intricately documented ritual procedures. Yet their lives were governed by a natural phenomenon which was beyond their control and was not entirely predictable – the inundation of the Nile. This was an event that tended not to be depicted: pictures of the landscape invariably showed the orderly state of the countryside once the river had returned to its normal course.

The creation myths envisaged the beginning of the world as the imposition of order on primeval chaos. The primordial waters of Nun symbolized chaos, while a sense of order was associated with the agricultural cycle and the passage of the sun. Maat, the goddess of truth and justice, also represented social and religious order, which maintained the equilibrium of the Egyptian world.

(36 x 54in) now in the British Museum in London. The inscription was commissioned by the Twenty-fifth Dynasty king Shabaqo (c.716–c.702 BC), who ordered it to be set up in the temple of Ptah at Memphis.

The introduction explains that the king ordered the story to be copied on to stone because the original was written on a material which was becoming very worm-eaten (presumably papyrus or leather), and thus difficult to read.

It was once thought that the language used in the inscription was typical of the Old Kingdom (c.2686–c.2181 BC), and that the original must date to this period. It is now agreed that the original was probably of the late Ramesside Period (c.1100 BC), or possibly even later, although Ptah was clearly regarded as a creator god as early as the Old Kingdom. In the Coffin Texts of the Middle Kingdom (c.2055–c.1650 BC), as well as in later Ramesside texts (c.1200 BC), he is deemed responsible for fashioning the gods and the sun, and for ripening the crops.

The thinking heart

In this myth it is clear that the heart is regarded as the organ for thinking. The ancient Egyptians were not aware of the function of the brain, and instead believed the heart to be the seat of both wisdom and emotion (the idea of thinking with the heart appears frequently). The fact that the brain was considered to be mere stuffing in the head is particularly well exemplified by ancient Egyptian funerary practices.

◄ Horus performs the Opening of the Mouth ceremony on the mummified body, restoring Sennedjem's senses and enabling him to be reborn into the Afterlife. From the tomb of Sennedjem, Deir el-Medina, 13th century BC.

last rite before emtombment, various ritual instruments were held up to the mouth and nose of the statue or dead body in order to ignite the senses and breathe life into the vessels for the *kas*. Ptah, the creator god of Memphis, was credited with having invented this particular ritual.

The modern name 'Egypt' derives from the Greek word for the country, *Aiguptos*, and it has been suggested that this in turn derived from the name of one of Ptah's temples at Memphis, *Hwt-ka-Ptah* (which means 'The Mansion for the *ka* of Ptah').

▼ Figures of bound captives were used in execration rituals. The potency of the magic was heightened by inscribing the name of the enemy (potential or actual) on the figurine. It is unusual for an execration figure to be female.

The potency of names

The idea of naming something in order to give it a life force is apparent here, as elsewhere in ancient Egyptian thought. The belief that the name was the essence of a deity's potency is clearly illustrated in the myth of *Isis and the Sun God's Secret Name*. In the world of mortals, 'Execration Texts' show that if the ancient Egyptians knew an enemy's name they believed that they could magically destroy him by writing it in a curse on a clay bowl or figurine in the form of a bound captive, which could be smashed as part of an execration ritual.

In the Memphite creation myth the initial concept of a god coupled with the

uttering of his or her name caused his or her vital force (*ka*) to come into being; this then required a vessel in which to reside. Most usefully the vessel would be a statue, because this could then act as the icon or focus of the cult.

Human beings were each believed to have their own *ka* which was represented in art as a person's double. On death it was thought necessary to preserve the body so that the *ka* (often translated as 'spirit') could survive. A similar ritual was performed on statues of gods and kings destined for the shrines and temples as was performed on mummified bodies before burial. In the 'Opening of the Mouth' ceremony, the

▲ *The cataract region of Aswan looks idyllic, but the granite rocks over which the river flows here can make navigation treacherous.*

The Background to the Creation Myth of Elephantine

Elephantine is an island in the centre of the River Nile opposite the modern town of Aswan, in the area of the first cataract at the southern border of Egypt. Archaeological excavations since the 1970s have established that it was the site of a large urban settlement, by at least the Roman period.

The city of Elephantine was the chief cult centre of Khnum, the ram-headed god. Here he was worshipped as part of a triad with his consort Satet (usually depicted as a woman wearing the white crown of Upper Egypt with antelope horns on each side) and their daughter Anuket (normally represented as a woman wearing a tall plumed crown and holding a papyrus sceptre), who was the goddess of the first cataract. Khnum's female counterpart was the frog goddess Heket, who was regarded chiefly as a goddess of childbirth, acting as a divine midwife at royal births. Just as Khnum fashioned the first humans on his potter's wheel, so Heket gave life to the unborn child by fashioning it inside the mother.

The Elephantine version of the creation myth appears on the walls of the Graeco-Roman temple at Esna in Upper Egypt. This temple survives only in the form of one hypostyle hall. Hymns dedicated to Khnum by his priests relay the premiss of the myth. The same theme can be found in the myth of the divine birth of the ruler, in which Khnum fashions the ruler and his or her *ka* from clay on his potter's wheel (see *The Divine Birth of the Egyptian King*).

Deities of the Nile

The creative force of the Nile was acknowledged in the worship of deities associated with the river. While Khnum was revered at Elephantine as a creator god, his consort Satet was associated with the annual flood, and daughter Anuket with the cataracts. Goddesses of fertility and childbirth were portrayed as Nile creatures, such as Heket, the frog-goddess and Taweret, the hippopotamus goddess. The chief deity of the Nile inundation was Hapy who was thought to live in the caverns of the cataract presided over by Khnum. Hapy was depicted as a man with a paunch and pendulous breasts. He often wore aquatic plants on his head.

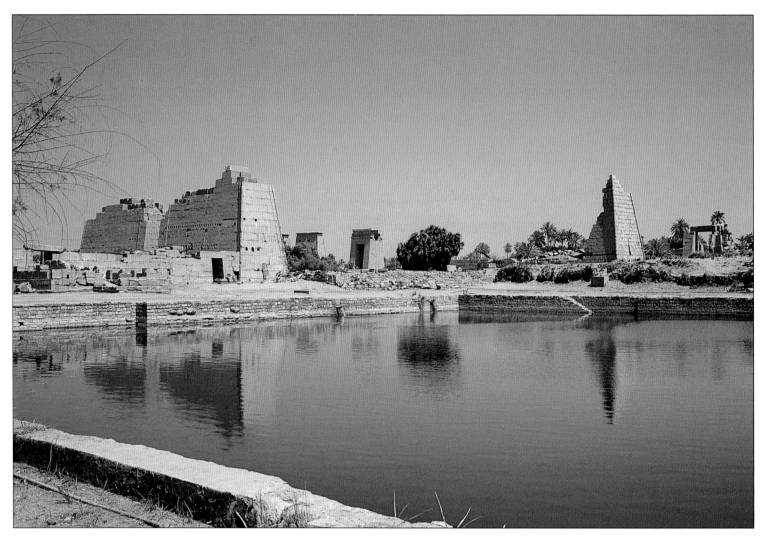

The Background to the Creation Myth of Hermopolis Magna

Hermopolis Magna (modern el-Ashmunein; ancient Khmun) is situated on the west bank of the Nile in Middle Egypt, close to the modern town of Mallawi. It was the chief cult centre of the god Thoth, identified by the Greeks with their god Hermes.

The earliest known version of this myth dates to the Middle Kingdom (c.2055–c.1650 BC). It offers a perfect example of the way a local deity associated with a specific theology could rise to national prominence when the centre of his cult grew in importance. In this case the god was Amun, who occurs in this myth as Amun Kematef ('he who has completed his moment'). At Thebes, Amun came to be considered as the supreme creator god, and his priesthood was able to surpass the king in power in that region.

Elsewhere, in representations of the sun god coming into being, the eight primordial deities mentioned in this myth are sometimes depicted as baboons in the posture of greeting the rising sun. This is a fine example of the way in which the ancient Egyptians made observations of the natural world and then incorporated them into the iconography of their religious beliefs. At dawn, baboons have a habit of sitting up on their hind legs with their front paws raised, in order to warm their undersides in the morning rays of the sun. This upright posture, with arms and hands raised in front of the face, was adopted as the posture of adoration by humans before the gods.

The numbers four and eight were considered magically significant by the ancient Egyptians. Both numbers were associated with totality, and so the creation of eight deities, in four pairs, makes sense within the context of the Hermopolitan idea of the cosmos.

▲ *The sacred lake in a temple complex such as Karnak would have been the source of water for libations and purification rituals.*

The city of Thoth

Thoth, the god of wisdom and writing, was the scribe to the gods and also their messenger. Because of this latter role, the Greeks identified him with Hermes. His city, Khmun, was therefore renamed Hermopolis ('City of Hermes') during the Graeco-Roman period.

Thoth was worshipped in this period under the name of Hermes Trismegistos ('Thrice-great Hermes'). He was believed to command 'the sacred books in the house of life', i.e papyrus rolls housed in temple libraries, inscribed with medical treatise, mathematical problems, etc.

The Background to the Creation Myth of Heliopolis

Heliopolis is a Greek name meaning 'City of the Sun'. The ancient Egyptians called the city Yunu or On; it is now known as Tell Hisn. It lies a short distance north of the ancient capital at Memphis, and today the site is built over as the area forms part of the north-eastern suburbs of Cairo.

The Ennead (nine gods) of the Heliopolitan myth occur for the first time in the Pyramid Texts of the Old Kingdom (c.2350 BC). Elsewhere the word ennead sometimes serves as a collective noun for gods. In the Pyramid Texts for example, all the gods of the Egyptian pantheon are described as the 'Two Enneads'.

The idea of the primeval mound emerging from the watery chaos is quite clearly an image borrowed from the natural environment – that of the floodwaters subsiding to reveal the deposits of fertile Nile silt. The ancient Egyptians built their settlements on the highest possible ground in order to avoid the damaging inundation. When the Greek historian Strabo (c.63 BC– c.AD 21) visited Egypt during the reign of the Roman emperor Augustus (30 BC–AD 14), he commented that as a result of the annual flooding of the Nile, 'the whole country is under water and becomes a lake, except the settlements, and those are situated on natural hills or on artificial mounds and contain cities of considerable size and villages which, even when viewed from afar, resemble islands' (*Geography* 17.1.4).

Once Atum has sparked off the process of creation, the myth hinges on the existence of male-female partnerships, and sexual intercourse is the catalyst for continued creation. It is interesting that the divine personification of earth (Geb) is male whereas in most other cultures earth is considered to be female. It is

▲ *When David Roberts drew the Colossi of Memnon in the 1838, the Nile still flooded annually, as it had done in ancient times. These two giant statues of Amenhotep III originally flanked the gateway to his mortuary temple in western Thebes.*

also noteworthy that all the procreative couples have brother-sister relationships, thereby providing divine stereotypes for childbearing marriages within the royal family, especially in the case of Osiris and Isis who were regarded as the archetypal royal couple. However, this incestuous arrangement seems to have been confined to royal couples, stressing their divinity and separating them from ordinary people: when non-royal husbands and wives (both lovers and married couples) referred to each other as 'brother' and 'sister', they appear to have been using these terms as expressions of affection rather than describing actual familial relationships. ◆

The Death of Osiris

During a time beset by turmoil, the birth of the god Osiris was heralded by an array of good omens and positive signs. Before his appearance, war and cannibalism appear to have been the order of the day – the people were said to be barbarians. Osiris became king of the Delta town of Busiris, but it was not long before he was made king of all Egypt. His skill lay in his ability to teach the unruly population to farm the land successfully and to lead law-abiding lives and worship the gods. Order had quite clearly been restored to the country when Osiris decided to go away on a journey and his wicked brother Seth seized the opportunity to gather together 72 conspirators. They hatched a treacherous plot.

On Osiris's return they threw a party and, following an enormous banquet, Seth suggested that the revellers should play a game (devised by him of course). A chest was laid out in the great hall and the game was to see who could fit inside it. When Osiris's turn came, he climbed

▼ In the funerary art, Isis (here on the left) and her sister Nephthys are often shown as kites.

into the chest, and – not surprisingly – it was the perfect-sized coffin for him.

One of the conspirators leapt forward and slammed down the lid, trapping Osiris inside. Unable to free himself, Osiris died and thus became ruler of the dead in the Afterlife.

This is by no means the end of the myth, however, because Osiris's dead body, still inside the chest, was disposed of in the Tanitic branch of the Nile. Its journey had only just begun, for instead of sinking to the murky depths as Seth had hoped, it floated with the current northwards towards the coast, and then out into the Mediterranean Sea. As if that was not far enough, it proceeded to bob all the way to the busy Lebanese port of Byblos, and finally came to rest in the entangled roots of a tree. Engulfed by the tree, the chest became part of its

▲ It is appropriate that this shrine of Osiris should resemble a coffin, as he was god of the dead and the Afterlife. In his myth he dies when he is confined in a chest by his brother Seth.

trunk. In due course the tree was cut down and turned into a pillar. Soon, Osiris's body was helping to support the roof of the palace of Byblos's ruler.

The quest of Isis

Meanwhile, Osiris's sister and consort Isis had set her heart on retrieving the body of her husband, in order to give it a proper burial in accordance with Egyptian customs. To make her searching easier, and fearful of her brother Seth's intentions, she hid her young child Horus in the Delta marshes, under the watchful eye of the protective cobra-form goddess Wadjet, who had her cult centre at Buto (ancient Pe).

Isis followed a tip-off to Byblos, where she befriended a group of the queen's maids and thereby gained access to the

◄ *In addition to faience examples such as this one, an enormous number of bronze figures of Isis suckling the infant Horus have survived from the Late Period of ancient Egyptian history.*

▲ *This papyrus illustration from the Book of the Dead of Lady Cheritwebeshet shows Seth protecting the sun god from the threat of the serpent-demon Apophis. 21st Dynasty.*

temple. Her magical powers (including turning herself into a swallow, and performing rituals to make the dead Osiris immortal) became known to the king and queen, who offered the goddess anything they might be able to give her. They presumably hid their surprise when she requested a certain column in the royal house.

Osiris's burial

Thus in possession of the chest, Isis returned to Egypt with it, and hid it in the marshy Delta while she went to collect her son. This proved to be unwise, because Seth happened to be out hunting that night in that particular vicinity, and no doubt could not believe his luck when he happened upon the chest. He proceeded gleefully to hack Osiris's body into 14 pieces (or more, according to inscriptions at the temples of Dendera and Edfu), scattering them far and wide.

It seemed as though Osiris's body was destined not to receive the burial it deserved, but Isis refused to give up and began her search for the strewn pieces. At each place that she found a missing piece, she conducted a burial ceremony (thus explaining the claim made by several of the ancient Egyptian temples that they housed the tomb of Osiris). Only one part of his body was never found, and that was his penis, which had been swallowed by a fish. In order to ensure the correct burial of Osiris's entire body, his dutiful wife made him an artificial penis.

So Isis was able to work her magic, not to bring her husband back from the dead, but finally to bury his dismembered remains. Meanwhile Osiris had taken up the position of king of the dead in the Afterlife. ◆

Osiris's gifts to humankind

As the son of Geb, the earth, and Nut, the sky, Osiris probably originated as a fertility god of earth and underworld. During his reign as king of Egypt, he taught his subjects how to make bread and wine, and oversaw the building of the first temples and statues to the gods. He built towns and set just and fair laws. Having civilized Egypt, Osiris embarked on a journey to repeat the process in neighbouring countries.

The Death of Osiris in Context

This version of the myth of Osiris is the one recorded by the Greek writer Plutarch (c.AD 46–c.126). He visited Egypt and was inspired to write an account of this age-old story (albeit with a Greek slant). He called it *Peri Isidos kai Osiridos*. There is no doubt that Plutarch was relating a truly Egyptian tale, but a survey of the various accounts of Osiris's death reveals a number of variations.

The legend of Osiris's rule over Predynastic Egypt was being written down from as early as the Fifth Dynasty (c.2494–c.2345 BC), but those references that survive in the Pyramid Texts really give very little detail. The king dies 'falling on his side' on the riverbank at Abydos (or Nedjet) but no cause of death is given. Early accounts do not mention the dismemberment of Osiris's body but they do tell us that Isis has to search for the body and, finding it, she 'gathers up his flesh' so that it can be embalmed at Abydos. The mention of this temple site is significant because throughout pharaonic history it was believed to be the burial place of Osiris.

The Coffin Texts of the Middle Kingdom (c.2055–c.1650 BC) inscribed, as the name implies, on coffins of this period embellish the story. They say that it was indeed Seth who killed Osiris at Nedjet, and Isis (together with her sister Nephthys) is said to have mummified the dead body.

Osiris's penis

A major variation on Plutarch's telling of the myth can be found in the Chapel of Sokar, in the temple built by the Nineteenth-Dynasty king Seti I (c.1294–c.1279 BC) at Abydos. It contains reliefs indicating that Horus

▶ *Osiris's false curled beard, as illustrated here in the tomb of Nefertari in the Valley of the Queens, is distinct from the false straight beards worn by the living pharaohs. 19th Dynasty.*

▲ This Roman period gilt coffin shows Isis and Nephthys mourning the death of Osiris. Isis is also portrayed as a kite hovering over the mummified body.

This myth is, however, particularly important because it provides a divine prototype for the practice of mummification, and for the concept of rebirth into the Afterlife. It was believed that Osiris's body was the first to be mummified, and the lengths to which Isis went in order to retrieve the various parts of Osiris's body and to give them a proper burial, weaving lengths of linen for the wrapping of the body, reflects the ancient Egyptian fear of dying in the desert or abroad in case this meant that they would not be buried in accordance with traditional funerary rituals.

The ancient Egyptians believed that in order to be granted a place in the Afterlife a person needed his or her body to be buried intact and should also have a suitable funeral, including all the correct spells and rituals. So this myth provides a model for ancient Egyptian funerary beliefs as well as for the concept of the deceased king of Egypt being identified with the god Osiris. It is also the prototype for brother-sister marriages within the royal family. ◆

had not been born before Osiris's death. In one scene Osiris is lying on an embalming table manually stimulating his penis. The relief on the opposite wall displays Isis in the guise of a sparrow-hawk hovering over Osiris's erect penis so as to be impregnated by him. Unlike Plutarch's version, in the pharaonic tradition Osiris's penis was not swallowed by a fish, but was laid to rest in the capital of Memphis (close to modern-day Cairo).

The idea of Horus as a young boy being hidden away in the marshes is evident in the pharaonic tradition because he is thought to have survived a scorpion sting while hiding. The ancient Egyptians believed that if children were stung by a scorpion they must identify them in spells with the child Horus, and this, it was hoped, would cure them.

Mummification

In the myth of Osiris, the belief, is evident that the gods ruled over the Egyptian people before the advent of the mortal dynasties.

▼ The fish motif, used in this glass vessel from Amarna, was common in ancient Egyptian art. 18th Dynasty.

Dying and rising gods

Osiris's death and the story of his grieving consort Isis contain elements common to myths about dying and rising gods in other cultures. All were associated with vegetation, fertility and the harvest, offering reassurance that their worshippers could rely on bountiful crops. They underlined the regenerative powers of nature, suggesting the continuance of future generations and, above all, the annual rebirth of the natural world.

Isis and the Seven Scorpions

The tale begins with Isis busily weaving the linen mummy wrappings for the body of her dead husband Osiris, who had been murdered by their brother Seth. She was interrupted by the god of wisdom and writing, Thoth, who advised her to take her young son Horus into hiding, in order to protect him from his uncle Seth.

Isis took heed of Thoth's words, and that evening she set off with an escort of seven scorpions. In order that Seth should not learn of their absence, Isis instructed the scorpions to be vigilant, and on no account to talk to any strangers on the way. Travelling through the Delta, they arrived at a place called the Town of the Two Sisters. There, rather than being welcomed by the local prosperous family, they had the front door slammed in their faces by the lady of the house. The scorpions were riled and vowed to wreak revenge. Six of them added their own personal supplies of poison to the sting of the seventh, who crawled under the rich woman's door and stung her young son almost to death. Beside herself, the woman rushed around the town desperately seeking help, but nobody responded to her cries.

It has been calculated that a mummy might be wrapped in up to 375sq m (450sq yd) of linen bandaging. This bandage bears a vignette from the 'Book of the Dead'.

A happy ending

Just as the boy was about to die, Isis intervened. She had been given lodgings by a peasant girl, and would not tolerate the death of this innocent child. To cure him, she held him and uttered a magic spell that involved naming each of the scorpions in turn, thus allowing her to control them. The event was to be life-changing for the boy's mother, who offered Isis and the peasant girl all her worldly possessions.

Egypt is home to two types of scorpion, the darker, relatively harmless Scorpioniae, and the paler, more poisonous Buthridae. The goddess Selket, shown here, took the form of a scorpion, and guarded the canopic jar containing the intestines.

Isis and the Seven Scorpions in Context

This story about the magical powers of Isis offered a means of curing, or protecting against the possibility of, scorpion stings. The same purpose is served by the myth of *Isis and the Sun God's Secret Name*.

The myth of Isis and the Seven Scorpions is found inscribed on the Metternich Stela, which is now in the Metropolitan Museum of Art in New York. This stone stela is a *cippus*, which means that it resembles a gravestone in shape, and has a central image of Horus as a child standing on a crocodile, clutching scorpions, snakes and other threatening creatures. Within this particular vignette the child Horus (Hor-pa-khered) is protected not only by the presence of the spirit deity Bes, but also by other deities and *udjat*-eyes, since the Eye of Horus was used as a protective amulet. A number of spells are also inscribed on the *cippus*, for use in a ritual in which water became imbued with magical potency when it was poured over the *cippus*. The liquid could then be ritually drunk or applied.

The recitation of the spell used by Isis in this myth was to be accompanied by a prescription of barley-bread, garlic and salt. Cereals, bread and salt are still used in Egyptian rituals today to appease and ward off evil influences. A poultice of barley-bread is also still used to draw out the poison when someone has been stung by a scorpion. The idea of sympathetic magic is very much apparent on the Metternich Stela: by identifying any child suffering from a scorpion sting with the young boy in the myth, they too could be healed.

Knowledge is power

As in the myth of *Isis and the Sun God's Secret Name*, the belief in the knowledge of a name giving control is an extremely important element. Isis can exert power over the scorpions only by naming them in her spell. The fact that there are seven scorpions is also significant, because the number seven was deemed to be magically potent and was used in various spells, particularly one involving the ritual tying and untying of seven knots.

Although healing spells derived from myths like this one often dealt with the most commonplace of problems, some of the most important of the Egyptian deities were involved in their solutions and remedies. So even the most superior of the gods and goddesses might play a part in the daily lives of the Egyptians, indicating how closely state and popular religion were interwoven. ◆

▶ *The magical potency of a Cippus of Horus was no doubt strengthened if it was held by a statue of a priest.*

Horus and the scorpion

Although Isis's magic was effective in counteracting the poison of the seven scorpions, she seems not to have had the power to cure her own small son, Horus. Having hidden him in the marshes at Khemmis in the Delta while she went to find food for herself, she returned to find that he had been stung. Her screams reached the ears of the sun god, Re, and caused him to bring his solar boat to a halt so that the earth was plunged into darkness.

Thoth left Re's boat and uttered a spell to cure Horus, threatening that the earth would remain dark until the poison left him. Horus was restored to health and Thoth charged the people of Khemmis with his care. Then he returned to Re's boat, which set sail again.

The Contendings of Horus and Seth

The myth opens with a courtroom scene and plunges straight into the deliberations of a trial that had already been dragging on for 80 years. This was, of course, no ordinary courtroom, but that of the gods, presided over by the sun god Re, and centre stage were Horus and Seth, who were there to contest the rightful claim to the throne of Egypt.

This long episode follows the death of the reigning king Osiris. The murder of this god, who had been maintaining a stable and prosperous rule over Egypt, was clearly the first step in a plan by his brother Seth to usurp the throne, but Osiris had died leaving a son and heir, Horus, who, it might be assumed, would have inherited the throne.

▲ *Neith wears the Red Crown of Lower Egypt. She was revered as 'mistress of the bow...ruler of the arrows'.*

▲ *Kharga is the southernmost and largest of the major Egyptian oases in the Western Desert.*

The indecision of the jury

The gods presiding in the court were by no means unanimous in their opinion. Some considered Horus too young to rule, and they believed Seth's strength would make him a more successful ruler. They were swayed by the fact that Seth travelled in Re's boat and repulsed the sun god's enemies, especially the serpent demon Apophis (see *The Journey of the Sun through the Netherworld*).

The divine court decided to turn to the advice and wisdom of the ancient goddess of warfare, Neith, who resided at Sais in the Delta. She was adamantly in favour of Horus, but was a fair arbiter and believed that Seth should be compensated with treasure and two Syrian goddesses, Anat and Astarte (described as Re's daughters). Her decision was coupled with a threat not to be taken lightly: if Horus were not allowed to succeed to the throne, the sky would fall down on the Egyptian people.

The gods appeared not to take this threat seriously because they still refused to agree on a final outcome. The argument was starting to get heated, especially when the deity Baba dared to insult Re by telling him his shrine was empty. The great sun god left sulking and returned only when he had been cheered up by his daughter Hathor, who made him laugh by exposing her genitalia to him.

A change of scene

The gods were beginning to get bored by the proceedings, so they decided on a change of scene. They relocated to an island, but Horus's mother Isis, who was particularly concerned that her son should inherit his father's throne, was believed to have a biased view, so the ferryman Nemty was forbidden to take her across the water from the mainland. But this goddess was a mistress of disguise and, transforming herself into an old hag, she fooled the ferryman into transporting her to the island. Once there she turned herself into a beautiful young woman and proceeded to seduce the unsuspecting Seth. She claimed to have been married to a cattle herder who had died, leaving her with a young son. She spun the piteous yarn further by telling him that a stranger had turned up and

▶ *The hippopotamus hunt depicted on the wall of the tomb of Mereruka at Saqqara symbolizes the victory of good, or order, over evil, or chaos, epitomized by the triumph of Horus over Seth. Old Kingdom.*

had tried to steal their cattle and throw her son out of their house. As Isis had hoped, Seth condemned the behaviour of this stranger, and in so doing, passed judgement on himself for his attempt to confiscate Horus's inheritance.

Horus was awarded the throne, but just as the matter seemed to have been decided, the proceedings became still more complicated and ambiguous.

Seth appealed and challenged Horus to an underwater contest, with both gods taking the form of hippopotami: if either of them was to surface before the end of three months he would lose his claim to the throne. Isis of course wanted to help her son as much as possible, so she decided to kill Seth and hurled a copper harpoon into the water. But the result was not as planned, for it accidentally embedded itself in Horus's flesh. Isis panicked, but was able to withdraw the weapon using magic, and threw it again. This time it hit Seth, but Seth reminded Isis that he was her brother and a pang of guilt caused her to withdraw the harpoon a second time.

Events grew stranger still when Horus rose out of the water, and in a fit of rage cut off his mother's head. She turned into a flint statue and he realized that he had overreacted. Fearing punishment he fled with his mother's head to the area of the Kharga and Dakhla oases in the Western Desert. But Seth was out to avenge his sister's decapitation. He tracked down his nephew lying under a tree, and gouged out his eyes (which, when buried, grew back as lotus flowers). It was left to the cow goddess Hathor to cure Horus's sight, which she did using gazelle milk.

The gods realized that things were getting out of control, so they summoned Horus and Seth back to court. But nobody could have predicted what would happen next.

A banquet was thrown during which Seth sexually assaulted Horus in order to humiliate him publicly,

▶ *Re, the sun god, was often depicted in his solar boat with a ram's head, wearing a sun disc on his head.*

and to display his own strength and superiority. The incident did not go as Seth had planned, however, because Horus managed to catch Seth's semen in his carefully positioned hands before it could enter him. He went running to his mother (whose head had been magically restored) with the rogue ejaculate. Shocked, she cut off her son's hand, disposing of it (and thus the semen) in the marshes. She realized that to foil Seth's plan completely he must now be tricked into ingesting Horus's semen, so Horus obliged (having had his hand magically replaced by Isis) and she spread some on Seth's favourite food, lettuce. Seth duly tucked into his doctored snack.

Back in the courtroom, the semen of the two gods was asked to speak out in order to ascertain its whereabouts and prove Seth's story about the assault. But instead of speaking from inside Horus, Seth's semen spoke out from the marshes, while Horus's identified itself inside Seth and emerged as a gold sun disc (indicating its divine origins) from the top of his head.

The final outcome

Seth was, of course, livid and challenged Horus to a boat race. Extraordinarily (although by now little should surprise us), it was decided that the boats must be made of stone. Horus craftily built his using pine painted to look like stone; Seth's (which was made out of a mountain peak) sank. Enraged, Seth turned himself into a hippopotamus and smashed up Horus's boat.

Enough was enough. Osiris sent a threatening message from the Netherworld and Horus was at last confirmed as the rightful heir to the throne. Seth's strength was not to be overlooked, however; he was employed by the sun god to thunder in the sky and to keep evil at bay.

Egyptian morality

The episode of Seth's homosexual assault on Horus seems to show him in a bad light, yet he had planned the whole episode to expose Horus by proclaiming the act himself before the gods' tribunal to help him win his case. The story would have been understood by the Egyptians in terms of the humiliating treatment of a defeated enemy.

Thus, when Horus's semen spoke from inside Seth, the general mockery was turned on him and he was seen as the defeated adversary. The New Kingdom Book of the Dead implies that homosexuality was condemned, but earlier texts suggest that homosexual relations were not considered morally wrong so long as there was mutual consent.

▼ *Wooden model boats were commonly placed in tombs of the Middle Kingdom Period. They might have oarsmen for heading north with the current, or sails when their journey was southwards with the wind.*

The Contendings of Horus and Seth in Context

This detailed version of the myth is found on a papyrus roll that has come to be known as Papyrus Chester Beatty number one (now in the Dublin Museum). It covers almost sixteen pages, and is written in hieratic script (the cursive form of hieroglyphs) by a scribe who had very fine handwriting. It comes from Thebes and dates to the Twentieth-Dynasty reign of Ramesses V (c.1147– c.1143 BC).

The Edfu reliefs

A more combative version of the myth appears on the walls of the Ptolemaic temple at Edfu, which is dedicated to Horus. In this series of text and relief it was Horus who, in the form of a winged disc, accompanied the sun god Re in his solar boat, and protected the sun against its enemies (which appear mainly as hippopotami and crocodiles, two animals that regularly threatened the safety of the ancient Egyptians).

In this version Seth was the leader of the pack of enemies, so he and Horus repeatedly came up against each other, taking various forms; for example, Seth was a cheetah or a snake while Horus was a lion. In the final showdown, Seth turned himself into a red hippopotamus. The battle took place at Elephantine, at the southern boundary of Egypt, and is said to have happened during a wild storm which churned up the river. In this way, an explanation is provided for the cataract at Elephantine – a granite outcrop under the water that turns that particular stretch of the river into a series of unnegotiable rapids. Horus triumphed by killing Seth with his harpoon. As Seth was dismembered, Isis decided that his bones should be fed to the cats and his fat to the worms.

The principal point made in this myth is that the son of the king should inherit the throne. The story provided a model for the smooth succession of the royal line. The aim was to protect the son and

▲ *The gods in the reliefs in the temple at Edfu, as elsewhere, were considered pagan by the Christians and were vigorously excised. Graeco-Roman Period.*

heir by providing a divine prototype – the living king would be identified with Horus, and the deceased king with Osiris. Seth played the possible usurper, who in reality may or may not have been a member of the royal family. The royal office was especially vulnerable when the son and heir was a minor on his father's death, as in the case of Horus, and when the alternative claimant was supported by a powerful court faction.

▶ *On the walls of the temple at Edfu, Horus wears the double crown of the pharaoh and harpoons Seth as a hippopotamus. Graeco-Roman Period.*

▲ *Temple reliefs and religious texts make clear the divine or magical properties believed to be held by breast milk.*

Courts of justice

The ancient Egyptians clearly believed that the divine world reflected that of mortals, and gods and goddesses behaved in much the same way as humans, for example in taking their disputes to court.

The important role of the court in ancient Egyptian society is well documented, particularly at the site of Deir el-Medina, the village on the west bank at Thebes inhabited during the New Kingdom (c.1550–c.1069 BC) by the tomb builders and their families. The local court was called the *kenbet* and its members were respected villagers joined by government officials connected with the community, such as a scribe from the vizier's office, which was based across the river in the main city of Thebes. The *kenbet* was mainly concerned with civil disputes between private individuals, especially over property and arising from economic transactions.

The vizier, who was the king's chief minister, presided over the 'Great Kenbet' or 'Supreme Court'. This was not a permanent assembly, but a selection of between eight and fourteen Theban VIPs who gathered when necessary to preside over the prosecution of particularly serious crimes, such as the tomb robberies of the late Ramesside Period (c.1100 BC).

Milk and lettuce

Both milk and lettuce have an interesting significance in this myth: Horus's eyes are said to be cured by the application of gazelle's milk, and it is said that Seth's favourite food, which is consequently drizzled with Horus's semen, is lettuce.

The milk used in the myth is that of a gazelle, but it is also true that human breast milk was considered an effective ingredient in medical prescriptions and magical rituals (although distinct in modern minds, the two were closely related according to the ancient Egyptian magico-medical texts). The milk of a mother who had given birth to a male child was considered especially useful for remedying colds, burns and eye diseases.

Similar cures continued to appear in the work of Hippocrates and of other classical writers such as Pliny and Dioscorides, as well as in Coptic medical texts and in European medical treatises up until the seventeenth

Sons and heirs

The throne of Egypt, having been granted to Horus, was thereafter known as the Horus Throne. Each successive king was identified with Horus while he lived and with Osiris, perceived as Horus's dead father, after his death.

The act of burying his predecessor, reflecting the service performed by Horus for Osiris, was enough to fulfil the new king's role as Horus and legitimize his position as son and heir to the throne. This could hold true even if the old king had not actually been his real father. If a king died without having produced a son, a successor – who might not necessarily be of royal blood – could validate his claim to the throne by burying the dead king. According to ritual, seventy days should elapse between the king's death and his burial, to allow for the funeral preparations.

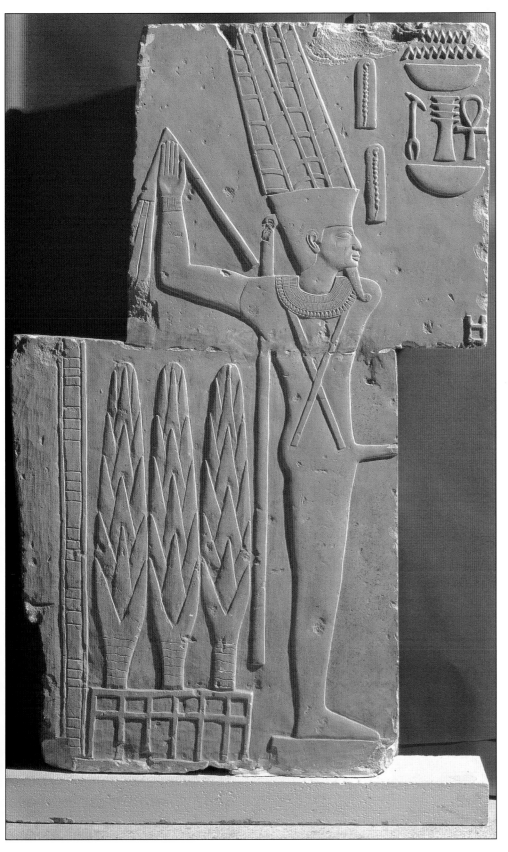

◀ *The tall lettuces behind the ancient god Min, on this fragment of relief from Koptos, were symbols of his cult and of fertility and sexuality.*

pot holds just over 100ml (4fl oz), roughly equivalent to the amount of milk produced by one breast at one feed. Perhaps the ancient Egyptians believed that when they put an animal's milk in such a pot, it magically became (or at least took on the therapeutic properties of) a woman's milk.

Lactating women were obviously considered in some way special in religious terms, because they were credited with *heka* or magic. A wet nurse might bear the title *Sau*, implying that she had a protective, safeguarding role, as *sa* was the word for 'protection' and also for 'amulet'.

The type of lettuce referred to in the myth is *Lactuca sativa longifolia*, which grew tall and straight like a modern cos lettuce and emitted a milky-white liquid when pressed. This fluid was presumably thought to resemble semen because the lettuce was closely associated with the fertility god Min, and the Egyptians considered it to be an aphrodisiac. Thus the choice of this particular vegetable in the context of this myth becomes more understandable.

In Egyptian folklore today, the lettuce is still considered an aphrodisiac. But classical writers had very different views on the effect the lettuce might have. Athenaeus stated that lettuce caused impotence; Pliny wrote that one particular sort of lettuce was called 'the anti-aphrodisiac' or 'the eunuch's lettuce' because it was 'an extremely potent check to amorous propensities' (instead, he recommended leeks as a sexual stimulant). Lettuce must have had a similar reputation in the seventeenth century as it was 'commended for Monkes, Nunnes, and the like sort of people to eate'. ◆

century. Even today, in Britain and other Western countries, mothers are commonly advised to treat their babies' eye infections with breast milk.

Some ancient Egyptian pots have been discovered that may well have been designed to hold breast milk. They are modelled in the shape of a breast-feeding woman or Taweret, the hippopotamus goddess of pregnancy and childbirth. Occasionally the pot has a hole in place of one of the nipples, which would presumably have acted as a spout. It has been calculated that each

The Destruction of Humankind

▲ *This gold statuette of Amun-Re holds an ankh, symbolizing the giving of life, in one hand, and the scimitar, a symbol of strength, power and foreign conquest, in the other.*

The events of this myth took place when the sun god Re was king of both the divine and the mortal worlds. He is described as elderly, with bones made of silver, flesh of gold, and hair of lapis lazuli.

The king learnt that humankind was plotting a rebellion against him. His immediate reaction was to destroy the race, but he felt he ought first to seek advice. He summoned his followers and ordered them to bring a number of deities to his court. Among them were to be Shu, Tefnut, Geb, Nut, Nun and, most crucially, a goddess he referred to as his 'Eye': this turned out to be Hathor in her peaceful manifestation, turning into Sekhmet when she became savage. The gods had to arrive secretly so that the human beings would not discover that their plot was being foiled.

The Eye of Re

The gods arrived at the palace and bowed before the king, who asked for their opinion on the matter in hand. Their unanimous suggestion was that he should send his Eye to slaughter the humans as they tried to escape into the desert. Re adopted their recommendation and the goddess readily obliged. However, after a day of massacre, Re was compassionate and felt that enough had been done to show humankind who was in charge. But the Eye of Re, as Sekhmet, was bloodthirsty and out of control: she was ready to wipe out the human race.

Now that the malevolent force of the goddess had been unleashed, Re had to find a way to restrain her. He sent swift-footed messengers to Aswan in the south to fetch a large amount of red ochre (a fine earth containing iron oxide,

▲ *This limestone statuette of a buxom brewer was placed in the tomb of Meresankh at Saqqara to ensure the production of beer for him in the Afterlife. 5th Dynasty.*

◀ One of the black granite statues of Sekhmet placed by Amenhotep III in the temple of Mut at Karnak. 18th Dynasty.

or haematite) and take it to his temple at Heliopolis, where the high priest was instructed to grind up the haematite. Maid servants were ordered to crush enough barley to make 7,000 jars of beer. This was to be no ordinary beer, but was to have the red ochre mixed in with it, so that it looked like blood. Work began immediately and continued throughout the night.

Could the human race be saved? Re rose early and ordered the fields where Sekhmet was due to resume her massacre to be flooded with the red beer. The goddess was ecstatic when she saw it, thinking she had happened upon a sea of human blood, and she gulped it down greedily. This had the desired result, and in her drunken state she did not even notice the people of Egypt, let alone continue to kill them off.

▲ Hathor's customary headdress was a sun disc sitting between cow's horns, but she was also shown wearing a falcon on a perch, as in this painted relief in the tomb of Horemheb in the Valley of the Kings, Thebes.

Re's abdication

Re had saved his people, and the frenzied goddess was once again peaceful. But the experience had been too much for the king. He decided he had had enough and abdicated, leaving the responsibilities of government to Thoth, the god of wisdom and writing. Re left Thoth to teach humankind the skill of literacy, and ascended into the sky on the back of the Divine Cow for a spell of peace and quiet.

The Destruction of Humankind in Context

Sections of this myth have been found in five of the tombs in the Valley of the Kings, on the west bank at Thebes. This particular royal burial site was employed by rulers of the New Kingdom (c.1550–c.1069 BC). The earliest example of the myth occurs on the interior of the outermost of the four gilded shrines that were found by Howard Carter in 1922 over the sarcophagus of the Eighteenth-Dynasty king Tutankhamun, (c.1336–c.1327 BC). The contents of this tomb are now in the Cairo Museum. There is a longer version of the text in a side-room off the burial chamber of the tomb of the Nineteenth-Dynasty ruler Seti I (c.1294–c.1279 BC), as well as variations of the text in the tombs of his successor

Ramesses II (c.1279–c.1213 BC), and two of the Twentieth-Dynasty kings, Ramesses III (c.1184–c.1153 BC) and VI (c.1143–c.1136 BC). Although all the known copies of the myth date to this particular period of Egyptian history, the style of writing is in fact that of the Middle Kingdom (c.2055–c.1650 BC), and so it is likely that it was originally written down at that time.

The myth is actually part of a longer religious text known as 'The Book of the Divine Cow', incorporating spells to protect the body of

◀ *The cobra goddess Mertseger ('she who loves silence') was known as the Goddess of the Peak. She commanded fear and respect among the villagers of Deir el-Medina, especially as she was believed able to cause blindness and venomous stings.*

▲ *The sky goddess could also be represented as a sow. A comparison was being made between a sow eating her young and Nut swallowing the sun and stars.*

the king and to ensure his safe ascension to the heavens. This was done by identifying him with the sun god, who rises successfully into the sky at the end of the myth.

The wrath of the gods

The main theme of the myth is, of course, the divine punishment of the human race, a theme which also occurs in the Mesopotamian and Biblical stories of the Flood. The significance of the image of a flood for the ancient Egyptians cannot be underestimated, but in this myth they are saved by it; their lives would have revolved around, and even depended upon, the annual flooding of the Nile that took place between July and October.

It is known from other sources that the ancient Egyptian gods were believed capable of meting out punishment to

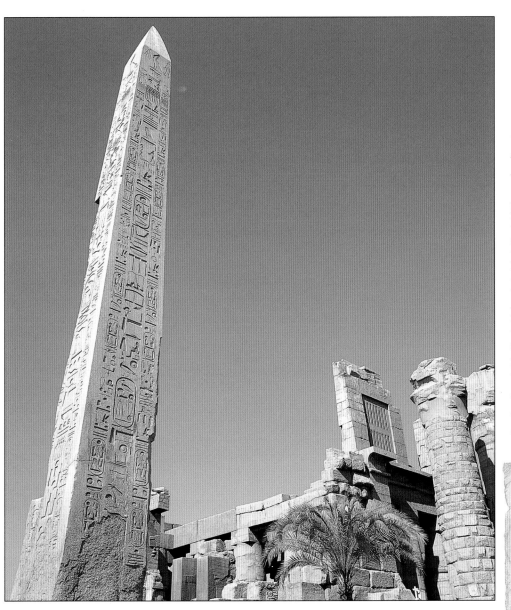

◀ *The original obelisk was the sacred* benben *stone at Heliopolis on which the first rays of the sun were said to have shone.*

past. In the early third century BC an Egyptian priest named Manetho was commissioned to write a history of Egypt by the Ptolemaic ruler of Egypt Ptolemy II (285–246 BC). Although he wrote his *Aegyptiaca* in Greek, he would presumably have had access to earlier Egyptian lists of kings, temple archives, and popular tales. Before dividing the rulers up into thirty-one dynasties, beginning with a king named Menes and ending with Alexander the Great, he described a period when gods had ruled over the Egyptian people.   ◆

Flood myths

A limitless ocean featured in the creation myths of many cultures as the primeval state of the world. A flood of global proportions was also a common theme, in which an inundation was sent to wipe out sinful humankind and restore the world to its pristine original state. The Egyptians believed that Re might well one day tire of humanity and that he had the capacity to return the world to the watery abyss of Nun.

Myths about overwhelming floods reflected the ambiguous nature of humanity's relationship with water, which was vital to life but also carried the threat of violence and devastation. In Mesopotamia, the Rivers Tigris and Euphrates flooded unpredictably, and their fearsome character was expressed in several versions of a flood myth which eventually found its way into the Hebraic tradition as the story of Noah's ark.

individuals for wrongdoings. The offences might be against specific deities (as witnessed by various penitential hymns found inscribed on stelae from Deir el-Medina), or they might be more general offences, such as the long list of wrongdoings that the dead had to be able to swear they had not committed in order to be granted a place in the Afterlife.

Born of the gods

But the gods were quite clearly merciful because it was perceived that their own existence was ultimately dependent upon the existence of mortals. The gods required the ancient Egyptian people to tend to them, provide them offerings of food, and build temples for them. A marked interdependence was evident – the gods were worshipped in exchange for their benefice.

Another reason why Re might well have had a change of heart when it came to wiping out all human beings was the fact that humankind had emanated from the sun god himself, that is to say from his tears, when he created the world. The ancient Egyptian love of wordplay and punning is conspicuous here, considering the similarity between the ancient Egyptian words for people (*remetch*) and tear (*remyt*). The magical association of similar-sounding words also occurs in the texts known as Dream Papyri. These were collections of dream scenarios that were thought useful for predicting the future.

The idea of the gods ruling over humankind is certainly not unique to this myth (see also *The Death of Osiris*), and was quite clearly crucial to the ancient Egyptians' understanding of their own

Isis and the Sun God's Secret Name

The sun god Re had many different names, but the one that held the key to his supreme power was a secret one that only he knew. Anyone lucky enough to discover the secret would be able to claim a position next to Re at the head of the pantheon of gods and goddesses.

Isis, who was very clever, was determined to discover this secret name so she hatched a plan. As an old man, Re drooled, and Isis collected some of his saliva and mixed it with earth to conjure a demon in the form of a snake, symbolizing Re's own strength.

Isis knew that Re was partial to a daily stroll outside his palace, so she familiarized herself with his usual route, and left the snake at the crossroads he was likely to pass. Of course he did walk this way, and the snake bit him, as Isis had intended.

The snake's venom entered Re and he became overwhelmed by a terrible fever. Because he had not created the snake, Re had no idea how to cure himself of the effects of its bite. He cried out in agony and the other gods came running but were unable to help him in his distress. His future was looking bleak, when Isis arrived. She offered to cure him on condition that he told her his secret name.

The sun god is cured

As well as being considered 'great in magic', Isis was known to have impressive medical skills, so Re was tempted, but he knew that having someone else in possession of his secret identity could put him in a vulnerable position. He tried to pull the wool over Isis's eyes by reeling off a long list of his other names, such as 'Moulder of the Mountains' and 'Maker of the Bull for the Cow in order to bring Sexual Pleasure into Being'.

But Isis could not be duped, and Re's symptoms grew even worse – he was sweating, shivering and losing his sight. In desperation, he agreed to Isis's bargain. He told her his secret name, but knowing that she would not be able to resist passing it on to her son, he insisted that she promise to make Horus swear an oath that he would keep the secret.

In receipt of this arcane knowledge, Isis became known as the 'Mistress of the Gods who knows Re by his own name', and recited a spell to cure the sun god's ailment.

▲ *Atum and Re appear as cats on this stela from Deir el-Medina. Below them, a married couple recite a hymn to the 'great cat' and the sun god. 19th Dynasty.*

▶ *The circular motif in front of this winged snake is a* shen, *the ancient Egyptian symbol of eternity. Valley of the Queens.*

Isis and the Sun God's Secret Name in Context

This myth survives on a papyrus dating from the Nineteenth Dynasty (c.1200 BC) which is now in the Turin Museum in Italy; a version of it can also be found in a more fragmentary state on another papyrus, Papyrus Chester Beatty XI, in the British Museum, London.

The main point of the myth was to emphasize the significance of a name, and the fact that knowledge of a name was equated with power. The ancient Egyptians believed the name to be very much part of the personality of an individual or the nature of an object. Generally, the myths served to provide the deities with their names and identities. It was not until a force had a name that offerings and prayers could be made to it by worshippers. But to know a name was to be able to exercise a certain degree of control over the deity (or person or thing) to which it belonged. Knowing the relevant names was particularly crucial in spells and their accompanying rituals (see *Isis and the Seven Scorpions*).

Mystery of the divine

It is significant that, in this myth, although Isis eventually managed to learn the sun god's secret name, the reader (or listener) never does. It was important to the ancient Egyptians that they could, to a certain extent, make sense of, and even identify with, their gods and goddesses, but by its very nature the divine world could not be completely familiar: it always retained a degree of mystery. The gods had to be believed to have their own secrets in order to inspire awe.

Magic and medicine

In this myth, Horus became party to the secret of the source of the sun god's power, so if the king was identified with Horus, he would presumably have been considered to be the only mortal with possession of this hidden knowledge, the key to certain powers.

The myth was obviously used in a ritual 'to ward off poison'. It includes the words of the spell with which Isis cured Re. Because she was successful in her combination of magic and medicine, it was thought that anyone suffering from a poisonous sting could be similarly cured.

As far as the ancient Egyptians were concerned, magic and medicine were not two distinct fields. The ten or so magico-medical texts that have survived show that spells and the use of amulets and other ritual objects were regularly combined with clinical observation and carefully worked-out prescriptions. This particular text stipulates that recitation of the spell is to be accompanied by a remedy of 'scorpion herb' mixed with beer or wine. ◆

Names

Egyptian names were chosen with care as they were considered to be an important aspect of a person's character. They might be derived from words indicating desirable qualities, such as beauty or wisdom, or from the names or attributes of gods to show devotion. Others associate the individual with the king.

From the Old Kingdom (c.2686–c.2181 BC) the king took five names, the first four of which he acquired when he came to the throne. The first was the Horus-name, or chief name. The second was the 'Two Ladies' name, giving him the protection of the goddesses Nekhbet and Wadjet. The third name, the Golden Horus name, referred to his divinity and the fourth, his throne name, introduced by the epithet 'He of the Sedge and the Bee' to his role as ruler. His last name, called the nomen, was the name given to him at birth and was preceded by the title 'Son of Re'.

▲ *The ideogram of a scorpion is one of the earliest known hieroglyphs; amulets in this form exist from the Old Kingdom.*

The Journey of the Sun Through the Netherworld

The sun god Re arose each day and, having bathed and fed, began his journey across the sky in his solar day boat. On the way, he spent one of the 12 hours of the day inspecting each of his 12 provinces, as he made a serene progression from east to west. During the night, however, he had to make a perilous voyage through the Netherworld while the land was left in darkness awaiting his return the following morning. The myth that describes his ordeal begins just as night falls.

The sun god had reached the western horizon, ready to begin his nightly journey through the Netherworld. He was all set to travel along the River of Wernes, a journey that would take him 12 hours.

In the first hour of the night he embarked on his journey in his night-boat with a crew of deities, including 'Path-opener' and 'Guide of the Boat'. He was also accompanied by two sets of nine baboons, who sang to Re as he entered the Netherworld and were there to open doors for him, as well as 12

▲ *The tomb of Tuthmosis III is painted with scenes from the Am Duat, 'The Book of that which is in the Netherworld'. Valley of the Kings.*

snake goddesses whose job it was to light up the darkness. In the second hour Re sailed on to the region of Wernes, where he granted land rights to the grain gods. In the third hour, he performed an important ritual act: he revived the god of the Netherworld, Osiris, by bestowing on him two divine forces described as 'Will' and 'Mind'. In the fourth hour, he reached a passage which was the way to

The fourth and fifth hours of night (the realm of Sokar) are shown on this sarcophagus. 30th Dynasty.

the underworld from the Gate of the Passageways, the entrance taken by the dead, and the route to the body of the hawk-headed Memphite funerary deity Sokar and the tomb of Osiris. The passage was guarded by a number of fantastic snakes with human heads and several short legs, or with wings and multiple snakes' heads.

The hazards of the journey

In the fifth hour, Re's solar boat was towed across a mound referred to as the Mound of Sokar, but in fact representing the tomb of Osiris and therefore flanked by his two sisters Isis and Nephthys in the form of kites. The tow-rope of the boat was held by a scarab beetle, symbolizing the coming emergence of Re from the night in the form of the scarab beetle deity Khepri. The entrance to the mound was guarded by four heads spurting flames, and even more extraordinary was a primeval embodiment of Re which appeared at this stage of his journey: Sokar balancing on a snake with a human head at one end and three snakes' heads at the other, emerging out of a mound of sand on the back of Aker, the double-headed leonine earth god. In the sixth hour, Re visited Thoth, the god of the moon, wisdom and writing, who appeared in the form of a baboon, but holding his other manifestation, an ibis. Thoth's role in this myth was to found a city for the gods and rulers of Egypt. Re also encountered an image of himself – the dung-beetle, in death

◄ A model or depiction of a boat was included in tombs to ensure that the deceased would be able to journey with the sun god in the Afterlife. 18th Dynasty.

the body of Khepri enveloped in the body of a five-headed snake.

In the seventh hour, Re sailed past enemies of Osiris (who his protectors were busily decapitating and lassoing with a rope) before coming face to face with his most terrible of enemies, the serpent demon Apophis, whose main aim was to swallow the sun. Re's magical protection allowed him to come into close contact with Apophis only if the demon was disabled in some way. Apophis had knives sticking into him, and in case this was not adequate disablement, the scorpion-goddess Selket held his head, and the 'Director of Knives' held his tail.

In the eighth hour, Re had to face further enemies, but luckily he had an entourage of human-headed staffs, each

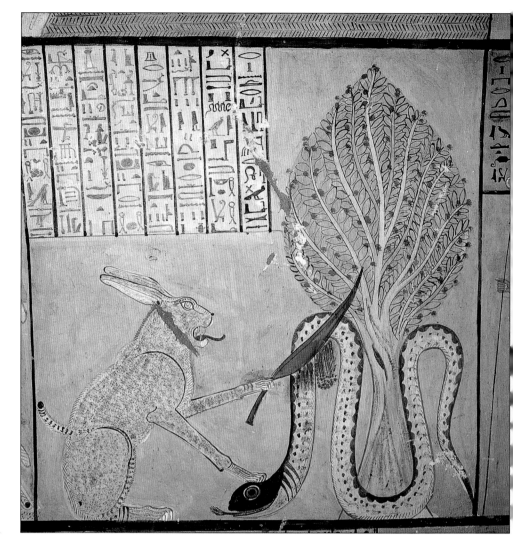

▲ *In this wall-painting in the Theban tomb of Inherkha, a knife-wielding cat slays the serpent-demon Apophis near the* ished-*tree. 19th Dynasty.*

▼ *This bejewelled winged scarab beetle rolling the sun with its forelegs, and resting its hindlegs on a basket, is the hieroglyphic representation of Tutankhamun's throne name Neb-Kheperu-Re, 'Lord of the manifestations of Re'. 18th Dynasty.*

of which had a knife with which to destroy Re's demons. A variety of deities, including gods with the heads of rats and mongooses, called out to Re as he passed their caverns. In the ninth hour, Re met the 12 alarming guardians of Osiris, fire-breathing cobras who lived on the blood of their captives. Decidedly less intimidating were the deities Re sailed past, who were responsible for carving trees and plants, and who held nothing more threatening than palm branches.

The end in sight

In the tenth hour, Re was beginning to prepare for dawn; he ordered his armed escort of 12 gods to seek out the last of his enemies, as he revealed himself as a scarab beetle, the manifestation of the sun god at dawn. In the eleventh hour, the hawk-god Horus presided over the final slaughter of the enemies of the sun god, which took place in pits of fire and was distinctly gory.

Re had survived the perils of the Netherworld, and the final hour before dawn had arrived. In the twelfth hour, the solar boat was towed into the body of an enormous snake, and the sun god emerged from its mouth as the scarab-beetle deity Khepri. Shu, the god of air, sealed the exit to the Netherworld behind him, and the sun god proceeded on his way in his daytime vessel.

The Journey of the Sun Through the Netherworld in Context

This particular myth of the nightly journey of the sun god is found in the 'Book of Am-Duat', or 'Book of What is in the Netherworld'. It is recorded in its most complete form in the Eighteenth-Dynasty tombs of the kings Tuthmosis III (c.1479–c.1425 BC) and Amenhotep II (c.1427–c.1400 BC), both of which are in the Valley of the Kings, the burial ground of the rulers of the New Kingdom (c.1550–c.1069 BC) on the west bank of the Nile at Thebes. In each instance the text is accompanied by a series of weird and wonderful painted images.

Similar, detailed descriptions of the journey of the sun god through the Netherworld are to be found in compositions entitled the 'Book of Gates' and the 'Book of Caverns'. The former can be found in its fullest version on the walls of the tomb of the Twentieth-Dynasty king, Ramesses VI (c.1143–c.1136 BC) in the Valley of the Kings, and inscribed on the sarcophagus of the Nineteenth-Dynasty ruler Seti I (c.1294–c.1279 BC), which was originally in his tomb in the Valley of the Kings but is now in the Sir John Soane Museum in London. The 'Book of Caverns' is the rarest and latest of the three funerary compositions, and it also occurs in its complete form in the tomb of Ramesses VI.

Darkness and death

The story identifies the journey of the sun during the hours of darkness with the passage of the dead (especially the king) into the Afterlife. Sunset is equated with death, and sunrise with rebirth. By recording the successful journey of the sun god in the tomb of the king, it was believed that the king would in turn be reborn without mishap. His enemies were regarded as the same as those of the sun god, and so it was important that they – especially Apophis – should be symbolically destroyed.

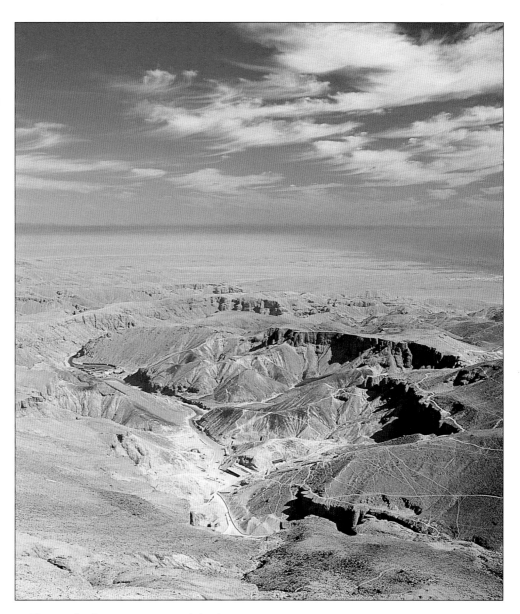

The myth also serves to explain the hours of darkness, so it is an alternative to the idea of the sun being swallowed by the sky goddess Nut in the evening, passing through her body during the night, and being given birth to by her in the morning. Other myths include the idea that the earth god Geb grew angry with his consort Nut for swallowing her 'children'. In the temple at Abydos, Nut is compared to a sow which eats its piglets.

The ancient Egyptians believed the Sun god to assume different manifestations at different times in the day. The most

▲ *The Valley of the Kings actually consists of two separate valleys: the eastern valley is the main royal cemetery of the New Kingdom, while the western one contains only four tombs.*

commonly occurring solar deity was Re, who tended to be associated with the midday sun. Atum was associated with the setting sun, and the scarab-beetle deity Khepri was the form taken by the rising sun. The fact that the sun god is imagined travelling in a boat should not surprise us because the chief means of transport both for people and goods would certainly have been by river. ◆

The Days Upon the Year

The myth is set at the time of creation, when the cosmological deities were coming into being. The sky goddess Nut was pregnant (following an illicit sexual encounter with the earth god Geb), but the supreme solar deity Re felt threatened by the prospect of the arrival of more gods and goddesses on the scene. He had convinced himself that his supremacy would be at risk if he did not take precautions, so he cursed Nut, preventing her from giving birth on any day of the year (which at this time still totalled 360 days).

As a result, Osiris, Isis, Seth and Nephthys would never have been born if Re had had his way. Luckily for them and humankind, the lunar deity Thoth decided to intervene. By beating the Moon in a board game, he managed to win enough light to create an additional five days each year (referred to by the ancient Egyptians as 'days upon the year' and as 'epagomenal days' by the Greeks). On each of these days, Nut was able to produce one of her offspring. To explain the existence of the fifth day, in this particular myth Nut is also said to be the mother of 'Horus the Elder' (Harwer; Haroeris in Greek).

The civil year

Even after the addition of the days upon the year, the Egyptian calendar did not coincide precisely with the solar year, which is 365¼ days long. The civil year gradually fell behind the solar year, moving backwards by one month every 120 years and only coming into alignment again after 1,460 years. As the civil calendar fell out of step with the seasons, festivals associated with the natural cycle (such as harvest) continued to be held in their correct season.

▲ *A scene from the Satirical Papyrus, showing a lion and an antelope playing* senet, *the best-known board game from ancient Egypt. Late New Kingdom.*

▼ *This cosmological vignette of Shu separating Nut from Geb comes from the Book of the Dead belonging to Nesitanebeteshru, a 21st Dynasty priestess.*

The Days Upon the Year in Context

This myth has survived in the work of the Greek writer Plutarch (c. AD 46–c.126), in a volume called *Peri Isidos kai Osiridos*. It was obviously originally devised as a means of explaining the five days which were added to the calendar in order to match it more closely to the solar year. The ancient Egyptians were in fact the earliest people to adjust their calendar to a length of 365 days.

Watching the stars

The New Year (*Wep Renpet*, literally 'the Opening of the Year') was celebrated when the dog star Sirius, the brightest star in the sky, was sighted on its heliacal rising. The Egyptians noticed that there was a 70-day period when the dog star could not be seen. During this time the earth, the sun and the dog star are so nearly in line that the light of the star is swallowed up in the sun's brightness and becomes invisible. At the end of this period is a night when, just before dawn, the dog star is momentarily visible just above the eastern horizon, an astronomical event known as its heliacal rising. It so happened that this usually took place at the time when the period of low water was coming to end, and it appeared to herald the inundation.

The Egyptians divinely personified Sirius as a goddess, Sopdet, depicted as a woman with a star on her head. They also created a god of the main southern constellation Orion, named Sah. Stars in general were often depicted as gods sailing on crescent-shaped barques through the body of the goddess Nut.

The calender

Initially, the Egyptian calendar was based on the agricultural cycle, which in turn revolved around the flooding of the Nile. The year was divided into three seasons, each of four months (each month averaged thirty days and was

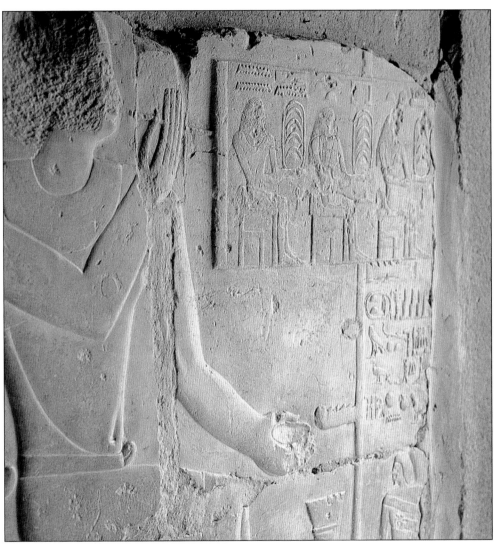

named after an important religious festival that took place during that period). The first season was that of the flood (*Akhet*), the second of planting and growth (*Peret*), and the last of the harvest and low water (*Shomu*). All three seasons were divinely personified as male deities.

The days of the demons

In the Calendars of Lucky and Unlucky Days, days were categorized according to the mythical events said to have taken place on them, and they would have been consulted in order to decide whether an activity should or should not be carried out on a particular day. The calendars made it clear that nothing of

▲ *The three seasons were divinely personified. Mereruka, the vizier of the 6th-Dynasty king Teti, is shown at the entrance to his mastaba seated before the seasons. Each is accompanied by four crescent moons symbolizing the four lunar months of each season. Old Kingdom.*

any consequence should be done on any of the 'days upon the year'. These extra days were added to the end of the calendar and did not form part of any month: all the months continued to be thirty days long. Of the five days upon the year, the one on which Seth was supposed to have been born was considered to be particularly dangerous, but all were collectively known as 'the days of the demons'. ◆

Trees in Egyptian Mythology

The shade of trees afforded the ancient Egyptian people welcome respite from the searing heat of the sun, so it is hardly surprising that sites associated with cults were often situated in groves. Soon the groves themselves came to be regarded as sacred and, according to various local traditions, gods were believed to shelter under, or even live in, particular trees. Trees were also important in the cemetery regions on the edge of the desert. But trees were relatively rare in ancient Egypt and this fact presumably heightened the respect in which they were held. There were no trees native to Egypt that could yield timber suitable for building work, so cedar had to be imported from the Lebanon for such uses as constructing ships and making roof beams.

There are two ways of finding out which trees were considered sacred in each of the nomes (or districts) of ancient Egypt. First, the emblems adopted by the nomes often include trees, and second, there are lists inscribed on the walls of Ptolemaic temples that describe the trees in each of the sacred groves around the country. The most common appear to have been the sycamore, persea (a sacred fruit-bearing tree), date palm and acacia.

Tallying the days

The hieroglyphic sign for 'year' (*renpet*) was a branch from a date palm with all the leaves stripped off (the notches left by the leaves were thought to indicate the passing of time). The presentation of a symbolic palm branch to the king was an important part of his jubilee festival, (see *Royal Jubilee Festivals*). Heh, the god of eternity, was depicted wearing a notched palm branch on his head or holding one in each hand.

Tree deities

Presumably because of the shade and the fruit provided by them, goddesses associated with protection, mothering and nurturing were closely associated with them. Hathor, Nut and Isis appear frequently in the religious imagery and literature. Any of these goddesses might be represented as a woman with a tree on her head, as a tree with the upper half of a woman growing out of it, or as a semi-personified tree with arms. In the tomb of the Eighteenth-Dynasty king Tuthmosis III (c.1479–c.1425 BC), a goddess (probably Isis) is depicted as a sycamore tree with a breast.

Hathor was sometimes referred to as 'Mistress of the Date Palm' (this refers to the male palm, *imaw*), and in the Book of the Dead the goddess was occasionally depicted in front of this kind of tree. She could also be called 'The Lady of the Sycamore' (the *nehet*, which also means 'refuge'), or more specifically, 'The Lady of the Southern Sycamore' – an actual tree that grew at the temple of Ptah in Memphis during the Old Kingdom (c.2686–c.2181 BC).

▲ *Nespawershefi, the 21st-Dynasty Chief of all the Scribes at Karnak Temple, is depicted making offerings before Nut, the sycamore tree goddess, on the side of his coffin. His* ba *is shown drinking the liquid poured by the goddess.*

According to the Book of the Dead, two 'sycamores of turquoise' grew on the eastern horizon at the place where the sun rises each morning, so the sycamore also had a male aspect as a manifestation of the solar deity Re-Horakhty. According to the Pyramid Texts, gods were thought to live in the branches of the sycamores on the eastern horizon.

In a funerary context, the goddesses Hathor and Nut occurred as sycamore tree goddesses, offering shade, food and water to the souls of the dead who, in the form of human-headed birds (*bas*), enjoyed the sustenance. The *bas* of the dead might be visualized sitting on the branches of a tree, rather as the gods were imagined on the eastern horizon. Sycamores were often planted near tombs, and models of leaves of this tree were used as funerary amulets.

The sacred ished

A tree that grew in the sacred groves of 17 of the nomes was the *ished*, a fruit-bearing, deciduous tree that was probably the same as the persea. Like the sycamore, it was associated with the rising sun and the horizon. And like the sun god, it was protected from the serpent demon Apophis by the 'great cat of Heliopolis'. According to the Book of the Dead, the cat that was said to sit in the shade of the *ished* tree was in fact Re himself. An inscription on the Heliopolitan obelisk known as Cleopatra's Needle in London records that a sacred *ished* grew at Heliopolis from the Old Kingdom through to the Graeco-Roman Period. (There were also *ished* trees at Herakleopolis, Memphis and Edfu.)

From the Eighteenth Dynasty (c.1550 BC), reliefs show Amun-Re, Thoth, the god of scribes, and Seshat, the goddess of writing, inscribing the leaves of the *ished* with the names and titles of the king and the number of years in his reign, so this kind of tree was associated with royal annals. The Egyptian word for 'records' or 'annals' was *genut*, from *genu*, meaning 'branch'.

Trees and rituals

The willow (*tcheret*), often identified as tamarisk, was sacred to Osiris. It was believed to have sheltered his dead body, while his *ba*, in the form of a bird, was said to sit in it. Those towns (including Memphis, Heliopolis and Herakleopolis) where part of Osiris was said to have been buried by Isis (see *The Death of Osiris*) had willow groves, and an annual festival called 'Raising the Willow' was celebrated to ensure the fertility of the land. Representations of the tomb of Osiris sometimes showed a tomb-chamber covered by a mound with trees growing on top of it or beside it.

Inscriptions at Philae record that milk was poured at the foot of trees at what was believed to be the sacred tomb of Osiris. These libations were thought to revive the god so that he might be reborn into the Afterlife. The reliefs show Osiris standing in a tree growing out of a small pool. An inscription at Philae describes Osiris's *ba* as living in the branches of a cedar tree while, according to Plutarch, a tamarisk shaded Osiris's tomb.

Deities were also associated with several other types of trees. The jackal-god Wepwawet was said in the Pyramid Texts to have 'emerged from a tamarisk bush', while Horus was believed to have come forth from an acacia (*shened*). In another myth, Horus was said to have taken refuge under an acacia tree as a child. A sacred acacia appears to have grown at Heliopolis. The crocodile god Sobek was associated with the *kesbet* tree and the moringa tree. Cypresses were deemed sacred to Min, and he was often worshipped under them.

Sacred trees are still important in Egypt. They are usually connected with the tombs of famous sheikhs, whose spirits are thought to dwell in them. They are believed to be able to cure problems such as infertility, and gratitude may be expressed by hanging votive gifts on their trunks. ◆

▲ *This semi-personified tree with a breast, suckling Tuthmosis III, is probably intended to be identified as the mother goddess Isis. Valley of the Kings.*

▼ *Another semi-personified tree offers food and drink to Sekeh, the deceased mayor of Memphis, and his* ba, *or soul.*

Plants and Flowers in Mythology

The papyrus plant (*Cyperus papyrus*) played a key role in the rise of the ancient Egyptian civilization because of the high-quality writing material that could be produced from it. The papyrus reed is a member of the sedge family and needs to grow in soft, easily penetrable soil, with its roots completely submerged in water. For this reason, the Faiyum and Delta districts were ideal habitats, and papyrus thickets were abundant in ancient times. As well as the fine sheets manufactured using strips of its juicy, starchy pith, the outer fibres of the papyrus plant were turned into boats, sandals, basketry, matting, boxes, ropes, jar stoppers and even building materials.

It is not surprising that the papyrus plant was highly prized. It was so closely associated with the northern region, that it came to be regarded as a heraldic emblem of Lower Egypt. In the iconography of the 'Unification of the Two Lands', a Nile deity or the god Horus might be depicted holding (or even wearing) this plant (see *The Concept of Duality*). Because it symbolized Lower Egypt and was believed to have grown on the primordial mound of creation, and in the belief that papyrus 'pillars' held up the sky, temple complexes usually included limestone or sandstone columns carved to represent single or composite papyrus stems, with capitals in the form of open umbels or closed buds.

For the ancient Egyptians, the papyrus plant also symbolized freshness, flourishing, youth and joy. To ensure the presence of these attributes in their lives, they would wear or carry a tiny amulet in the shape of a single stem and umbel of papyrus. It was stipulated that this should be made of green or blue-green faience, and it was referred to as *wadj* (literally 'green'). Goddesses such as Hathor, Bastet and Neith were often depicted holding a papyriform sceptre.

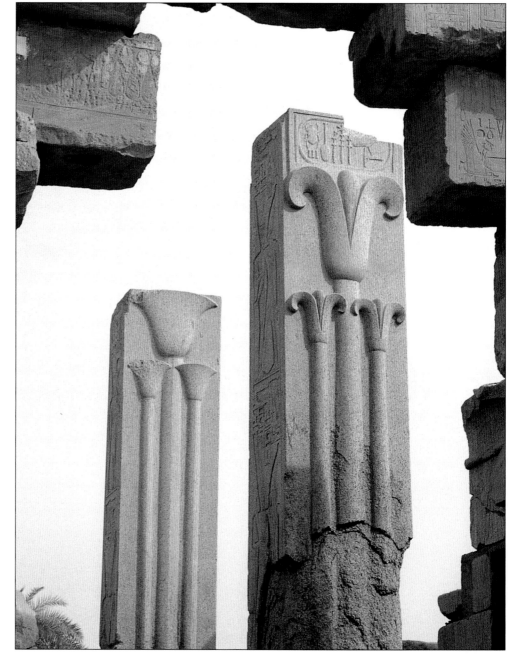

Lotus or lily?

The symbol of the South (Upper Egypt) is generally referred to as the lotus, but was actually the water lily (sometimes called the 'southern plant'). There were two species of lotus or water lily that grew in ancient Egypt, the white *Nymphaea lotus*, and the blue *Nymphaea caerulea*. It was the latter species that was most commonly depicted and was usually described as the sacred lotus. It

▲ *These two red granite pillars form part of the barque sanctuary of Tuthmosis III at Karnak. The pillar in the foreground depicts the lotus/lily and the other the papyrus plant.*

too occurs in the imagery of the 'Unification of the Two Lands', held (or worn) by a Nile deity or by Seth. Because of its significance, the sacred lotus was also an important element in the design of temple columns.

Flowers of life and death

During the New Kingdom the flowers of the *ished* tree were considered life-giving and were called 'flowers of life'. Together with the lotus blossom they were used at funerals for decorating the coffins and statues of the deceased.

The ancient Egyptians observed that the lily flower closed for the night and sank under the water, rising and reopening as the sun rose, and for this reason it was associated with the night-time journey of the sun god Re and his 'rebirth' at dawn. In time it came to be associated with creation and rebirth in general. One version of the creation myth of Hermopolis Magna tells us that the sun rose for the first time out of a primordial lotus bobbing on the waters of chaos (see *Creation Myths*).

Throughout Egyptian history images were created of figures rising out of lotus blossoms, such as the wonderful painted wooden head of Tutankhamun found in his tomb and now in the Cairo Museum. The lotus became so important

▶ *This wooden sculpture of Tutankhamun's head emerging from a lotus blossom has been plastered and then painted. The image likens the boy king to the sun god rising out of a lotus, in accordance with the mythology of creation.*

in ancient Egyptian religion that it was divinely personified in the form of the god Nefertem, 'Lord of Perfumes', who was portrayed anthropomorphically with a lotus growing out of his head (sometimes with two tall plumes extending upwards out of the flower). In the Pyramid Texts of the Old Kingdom Nefertem is described as 'the lotus at the nose of Re', and gods and goddesses are often depicted sniffing lotus blossoms.

Gods and flowers

Deities as well as people were thought to love the pleasurable stimulation of their senses, and flowers were considered to be important offerings to the gods.

We know that the sense of smell was highly regarded by the ancient Egyptians – the nose was the hieroglyphic sign used as a determinative in the writing of the verbs 'to enjoy' and 'to take pleasure in'. Flowers are ubiquitous in the scenes of festivity on the walls of Theban private tombs of the New Kingdom (c.1550–c.1069 BC). They are shown as festoons and garlands worn by the merry-makers, but are also depicted being held to the nose for the pleasure of their scent. It is likely that when added to alcohol they would have released psychoactive properties.

Certain plants were particularly associated with certain deities. The lettuce (*Lactuca sativa longifolia*) was, for example, an emblem of the cult of the fertility god Min at Koptos. This association may have arisen from the resemblance of the milky juice of the lettuce to semen (see *The Contendings of Horus and Seth*). ◆

◀ *The heavy black wigs and fine white linen dresses of these women, together with an abundance of flowers, are typical of the banqueting scenes on the walls of non-royal Theban tombs of the New Kingdom.*

The Concept of Duality

The crux of the ancient Egyptian system of beliefs was the relationship between order (*maat*) and chaos (*isfet*). Although a state of order was considered to be the ideal, it was acknowledged that an opposing yet interdependent state of chaos must exist in order for equilibrium to be achieved. For the ancient Egyptians, a state of order (or harmony or balance) was of such vital significance in their lives that they divinely personified the abstract concept of order in the form of the goddess Maat. She was represented as a woman wearing an ostrich feather, which represented truth, on her head.

A sense of unity was created by the existence of a duality, which was expressed clearly in religious iconography. The god Horus was associated with all that was right and ordered, whereas the god Seth was linked with chaos, as well as with infertility and aridity (see *The Contendings of Horus and Seth*). The presence of both of these deities indicated an idea of

▶ *Maat, the goddess of order, wearing an ostrich feather on her head, is characteristically shown seated on a plinth. The symbol of the plinth is included in the hieroglyphic writing of her name and represents the primeval mound of creation.*

completeness. In the Cairo Museum there is an impressive triad statue which was found at Medinet Habu, the mortuary temple of the Twentieth-Dynasty king Ramesses III (c.1184–c.1153 BC). The king is shown flanked by Horus on one side and Seth on the other – the two gods together constituting a wholeness.

The ancient Egyptians believed that the fertile part of Egypt (the Nile Valley and the Delta) in which they lived was a place of order with a reliable pattern to it – particularly the agricultural cycle hingeing on the annual flooding of the Nile. Maat was present in this, the 'Black Land' (*Kemet*). On the other hand, the desert or 'Red Land' (*Deshret*) was considered to be a place of chaos. A precarious, yet highly important, relationship existed between the two.

Unification

The conventions of Egyptian art were perfect for illustrating the concept of duality, because symmetry was frequently used to create a balanced design. This is best exemplified by the artistic representation of the fundamentally important idea of the 'Unification of the Two Lands' (*sema tawy*). The ancient Egyptians viewed their country as consisting of two distinct parts: Upper Egypt (*Shemau*) and

The two crowns

The Red Crown of Lower Egypt had a tall, thin back and a narrow coil that protruded at the front. It was the customary headdress of the northern goddess Neith, and its earliest known appearance is on a Predynastic pot from Naqada.

The White Crown of Upper Egypt was shaped like a tall cone with a bulbous tip. It was sometimes adorned with two plumes in a form called the *atef-*crown, which was associated with the god Osiris. It was placed inside the Red Crown to form the Double Crown.

Lower Egypt (*Ta-Mehu*). These correspond to the South (the Nile Valley from the first cataract north to just south of Memphis) and the North (the Delta), respectively. The people believed that the origins of the state of Egypt could be traced to an act of unification of these two regions by a ruler named Menes (for whom there is no actual archaeological evidence) at the beginning of the early Dynastic Period (c.3100 BC).

The hieroglyphic sign used to express the notion of this unification was a stylized rendering of a pair of lungs, with a windpipe extending straight upwards out of the middle of them. In art this emblem might be flanked by two deities, sometimes Horus and Seth, on other occasions two Nile gods, one with papyrus on his head and the other with the lotus (or water lily) plant (see *Plants and Flowers in Mythology*). The figures on each side are often depicted tying the papyrus and lotus stems in a knot around the hieroglyph. This is further symbolic of the unity of Egypt because the papyrus plant was a heraldic emblem of the Delta, and the lotus was a heraldic emblem of the Nile Valley.

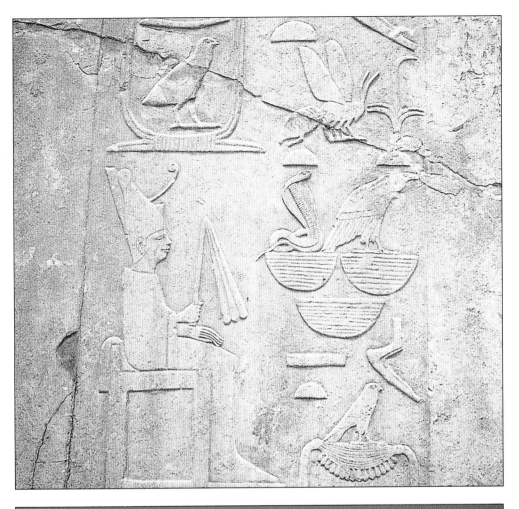

▶ *Snofru sits beneath his cartouche wearing the Double Crown of Upper and Lower Egypt. One of his chief titles, 'He of the Sedge and the Bee', is easily identifiable, and beneath this is his 'Two Ladies' epithet.*

Lord of the two lands

This particular aspect of the notion of duality manifested itself very clearly in the royal titles. The king's chief titles were 'Lord of the Two Lands' (*Neb Tawy*) and 'King of Upper and Lower Egypt' (*Nesw Bity*), which translates literally as 'He of the Sedge and the Bee'. The sedge plant was an emblem of the Nile Valley, and the bee was an emblem of the Delta. Another of his titles was 'He of the Two Ladies' (*Nebty*), which referred to the two goddesses who were thought to protect him: the vulture goddess, Nekhbet, who had her main cult centre at el-Kab in the South, and the cobra goddess, Wadjet, whose principal cult centre was at Buto in the North.

The regalia of kingship also reflected the idea of duality. The king might be depicted wearing the White Crown (*Hedjet*) associated with Upper Egypt, the Red Crown (*Deshret*) of Lower Egypt, or sometimes the Double Crown (*Pschent* or *Sekhemty*), which incorporated the crowns of both regions.

So north and south were distinct but both were necessary to create a whole. Similarly east and west were opposing and yet interdependent. The places of the rising and setting sun resulted in the east being associated with the living, and the west being associated with the dead. But as the sun rose again each morning, so the dead were believed to be reborn into the Afterlife. ◆

▶ *This diadem was found under the bandaging on Tutankhamun's mummy. For safekeeping, the cobra had been detached and placed on Tutankhamun's left thigh, and the vulture on his right thigh.*

Kingship and the Gods

D id the ancient Egyptian people believe that their king was a god? The extent to which they did seems to have varied according to the period of Egyptian history, and also to have depended on context. The king could be regarded as a god, or as somewhere between the divine and mortal world, or as a mere human being. It is safe to say, however, that the concept of kingship – the office, rather than the man himself – was considered divine. It was felt that the king could relate to the gods in a way that none of his subjects would have been able to, which must have enhanced the nature of kingship and inspired respect, if not awe, in the people.

Many sources reveal that the king was identified with a god, both in life and after death. Myths, inscriptions and royal titles all stress the reigning king's identification with the falcon-god Horus. After death, the king was identified with Osiris. The divinity of a dead king was less ambiguous than that of a living one, and is well attested throughout Egyptian history. By the New Kingdom (c.1550– c.1069 BC), the royal mortuary temples were on a par (in terms of size, wealth and administration) with the cult temples of the deities.

◀ *On the wall of a corridor in the temple of Seti I at Abydos, this king and his son, Ramesses II, stand before a list of cartouches representing their royal predecessors.*

Kings of Egypt

All dates are BC unless stated otherwise

Early Dynastic Period   c.3100–c.2686

FIRST DYNASTY	c.3100–c.2890
Narmer	c.3100
Aha	c.3100
Djer	c.3000
Djet	c.2980
Den	c.2950
[Queen Merneith	c.2950]
Anedjib	c.2925
Semerkhet	c.2900
Qa'a	c.2890
SECOND DYNASTY	c.2890–c.2686
Hetepsekhemwy	c.2890
Raneb	c.2865
Nynetjer	
Weneg	
Sened	
Peribsen	c.2700
Khasekhemwy	c.2686

Old Kingdom   c.2686–c.2181

THIRD DYNASTY	c.2686–c.2613
Sanakht (= Nebka?)	c.2686–c.2667
Djoser (Netjerikhet)	c.2667–c.2648
Sekhemkhet	c.2648–c.2640
Khaba	c.2640–c.2637
Huni	c.2637–c.2613
FOURTH DYNASTY	c.2613–c.2494
Sneferu	c.2613–c.2589
Khufu (Cheops)	c.2589–c.2566
Djedefre (Radjedef)	c.2566–c.2558
Khafre (Chephren)	c.2558–c.2532
Menkaure (Mycerinus)	c.2532–c.2503
Shepseskaf	c.2503–c.2494
FIFTH DYNASTY	c.2494–c.2345
Userkaf	c.2494–c.2487
Sahure	c.2487–c.2475
Neferirkare	c.2475–c.2455
Shepseskare	c.2455–c.2448
Raneferef	c.2448–c.2445
Niuserre	c.2445–c.2421
Menkauhor	c.2421–c.2414
Djedkare	c.2414–c.2375
Unas (Wenis)	c.2375–c.2345
SIXTH DYNASTY	c.2345–c.2181
Teti	c.2345–c.2323
Userkare	c.2323–c.2321
Pepi I (Meryre)	c.2321–c.2287
Merenre	c.2287–c.2278
Pepi II (Neferkare)	c.2278–c.2184
Nitiqret	c.2184–c.2181

First Intermediate Period   c.2181–c.2055

SEVENTH AND EIGHTH DYNASTIES	c.2181–c.2125
Numerous short reigns	
NINTH AND TENTH DYNASTIES (HERAKLEOPOLITAN)	c.2160–c.2025
Khety (Meryibre)	
Khety (Wahkare)	
Merykare	
Ity	
ELEVENTH DYNASTY (THEBES)	c.2125–c.2055
[Mentuhotep I ('Tepy-aa')]	
Intef I (Sehertawy)	c.2125–c.2112
Intef II (Wahankh)	c.2112–c.2063
Intef III (Nakhtnebtepnefer)	c.2063–c.2055

Middle Kingdom   c.2055–c.1650

ELEVENTH DYNASTY (ALL EGYPT)	c.2055–c.1985
Mentuhotep II (Nebhepetre)	c.2055–c.2004
Mentuhotep III (Sankhkare)	c.2004–c.1992
Mentuhotep IV (Nebtawyre)	c.1992–c.1985
TWELFTH DYNASTY	c.1985–c.1795
Amenemhat I (Sehetepibre)	c.1985–c.1955
Senusret I (Kheperkare)	c.1965–c.1920
Amenemhat II (Nubkaure)	c.1922–c.1878
Senusret II (Khakheperre)	c.1880–c.1874
Senusret III (Khakaure)	c.1874–c.1855
Amenemhat III (Nimaatre)	c.1855–c.1808
Amenemhat IV (Maakherure)	c.1808–c.1799
Queen Sobekneferu (Sobekkare)	c.1799–c.1795
THIRTEENTH DYNASTY	1795–after 1650

About 70 rulers, of whom the most frequently mentioned are
listed below

Hor (Awibre)	
Khendjer (Userkare)	
Sobekhotep III (Sekhemrasewadjtawy)	
Neferhotep I (Khasekhemre)	
Sobekhotep IV (Khaneferre)	c.1725
FOURTEENTH DYNASTY	c.1750–c.1650

Series of minor rulers, probably contemporary with the kings
of the Thirteenth Dynasty

Second Intermediate Period   c.1650–c.1550

FIFTEENTH DYNASTY (HYKSOS)	c.1650–c.1550
Salitis	
Khyan (Seuserenre)	c.1600
Apepi (Aauserre)	c.1555
Khamudi	
SIXTEENTH DYNASTY	c.1650–c.1550

Minor Hyksos rulers, contemporary with the kings of the
Fifteenth Dynasty

SEVENTEENTH DYNASTY	c.1650–c.1550

Several rulers based in Thebes, of whom the most prominent
are listed below

Intef (Nubkheperre)	
Taa I (Senakhtenre)	
Taa II (Seqenenre)	c.1560
Kamose (Wadjkheperre)	c.1555–c.1550

New Kingdom   c.1550–c.1069

EIGHTEENTH DYNASTY	c.1550–c.1295
Ahmose (Nebpehtyre)	c.1550–c.1525
Amenhotep I (Djeserkare)	c.1525–c.1504
Tuthmosis I (Aakheperkare)	c.1504–c.1492
Tuthmosis II (Aakheperenre)	c.1492–c.1479
Tuthmosis III (Menkhpererre)	c.1479–c.1425
Hatshepsut (Maatkare)	c.1473–c.1458
Amenhotep II (Aakheperure)	c.1427–c.1400

Tuthmosis IV (Menkheperure)   c.1400–c.1390
Amenhotep III (Nebmaatre)   c.1390–c.1352
Amenhotep IV/Akhenaten
(Neferkheperurawaenre)   c.1352–c.1336
Nefernefruaten (Smenkhkare)   c.1338–c.1336
Tutankhamun (Nebkheperure)   c.1336–c.1327
Ay (Kheperkheperure)   c.1327–c.1323
Horemheb (Djeserkheperure)   c.1323–c.1295
NINETEENTH DYNASTY   c.1295–c.1186
Ramesses I (Menpehtyre)   c.1295–c.1294
Seti I (Menmaatre)   c.1294–c.1279
Ramesses II (Usermaatra Setepenre)   c.1279–c.1213
Merenptah (Baenre)   c.1213–c.1203
Amenmessu (Menmire)   c.1203–c.1200
Seti II (Userkheperur Setepenre)   c.1200–c.1194
Saptah (Akhenra Setepenre)   c.1194–c.1188
Tausret (Sitrameritamun)   c.1188–c.1186
TWENTIETH DYNASTY   c.1186–c.1069
Sethnakhte (Userkhaure Meryamun)   c.1186–c.1184
Ramesses III (Usermaatre Meryamun)   c.1184–c.1153
Ramesses IV (Hekamaatre Setepenamun)   c.1153–c.1147
Ramesses V (Usermaatre Sekheperenre)   c.1147–c.1143
Ramesses VI (Nebmaatre Meryamun)   c.1143–c.1136
Ramesses VII (Usermaatre
Setepenre Meryamun)   c.1136–c.1129
Ramesses VIII (Usermaatre Akhenamun)   c.1129–c.1126
Ramesses IX (Neferkare Setepenre)   c.1126–c.1108
Ramesses X (Khepermaatre Setepenre)   c.1108–c.1099
Ramesses XI (Menmaatre Setepenptah)   c.1099–c.1069

Third Intermediate Period   c.1069–c.747

TWENTY-FIRST DYNASTY
(TANITE)   c.1069–c.945
Smendes (Hedjkheperre Setepenre)   c.1069–c.1043
Amenemnisu (Neferkare)   c.1043–c.1039
Psusennes I [Pasebakhaenniut]
(Aakheperre Setepenamun)   c.1039–c.991
Amenemope (Usermaatre Setepenamun)   c.993–c.984
Osorkon the Elder (Aakheperre Setepenre)   c.984–c.978
Siamun (Netjrkheperre Setepenamun)   c.978–c.959
Psusennes II [Pasebakhaennuit]
(Titkheperure Setepenre)   c.959–c.945
TWENTY-SECOND DYNASTY
(BUBASTITE/LIBYAN)   c.945–c.715
Sheshonq I (Hedjkheperre Setepenre)   c.945–c.924
Osorkon I (Sekhemkheperre)   c.924–c.889
Sheshonq II (Hekakheperre Setepenre)   c.890
Takelot I   c.889–c.874
Osorkon II (Usermaatre Setepnamun)   c.874–c.850
Takelot II (Hedjkheperre Setepenre amun)   c.850–c.825
Sheshonq II (Usermaatre)   c.825–c.773
Pimay (Usermaatre)   c.773–c.767
Sheshonq V (Aakheperre)   c.767–c.730
Osorkon IV (Aakheperre Setepenamun)   c.730–c.715
TWENTY-THIRD DYNASTY
(TANITE/LIBYAN)   c.818–c.715
Several contemporary lines of rulers at Herakleopolis Magna,
Hermopolis Magna, Leontopolis and Tanis, three of whom are
listed below
Pedubastis I (Usermaatre)   c.818–c.793
Sheshonq IV   c.780
Osorkon III (Usermaatre Setepenamun)   c.777–c.749
TWENTY-FOURTH DYNASTY   c.727–c.715
Bakenrenef (Bocchoris)   c.727–c.715

Late Period   c.747–332

TWENTY-FIFTH DYNASTY
(KUSHITE)   c.747–c.656
Piy (Piankhy)   c.747–c.716
Shabaqo (Neferkare)   c.716–c.702
Shabitqo (Djedkaure)   c.702–690
Taharqo (Khunefertemre)   690–664
Tanutamani (Bakare)   664–656
TWENTY-SIXTH DYNASTY
(SAITE)   664–525
[Nekau I   672–664]
Psamtek I (Wahinre)   664–610
Nekau II (Wehemibre)   610–595
Psamtek II (Neferibre)   595–589
Apries (Haaibre)   589–570
Ahmose II (Khnemibre)   570–526
Psamtek III (Ankhkaenre)   526–525
TWENTY-SEVENTH DYNASTY
(FIRST PERSIAN PERIOD)   525–404
Cambyses   525–522
Darius I   522–486
Xerxes I   486–465
Artaxerxes I   465–424
Darius II   424–405
Artaxerxes II   405–359
TWENTY-EIGHTH DYNASTY   404–399
Amyrtaios   404–399
TWENTY-NINTH DYNASTY   399–380
Nepherites I   399–393
Hakor (Khnemmaatre)   393–380
Nepherites II   c.380
THIRTIETH DYNASTY   380–343
Nectanebo I (Kheperkare)   380–362
Teos (Irmaatenre)   362–360
Nectanebo II (Senedjemibre Setepenanhur)   360–343
SECOND PERSIAN PERIOD   343–332
Artaxerxes III Ochus   343–338
Arses   338–336
Darius III Codoman   336–332

Ptolemaic Period   332–30

MACEDONIAN DYNASTY   332–305
Alexander the Great   332–323
Philip Arrhidaeus   323–317
Alexander IV   317–310
PTOLEMAIC DYNASTY
Ptolemy I Soter I   305–285
Ptolemy II Philadelphus   285–246
Ptolemy III Euergetes I   246–221
Ptolemy IV Philopator   221–205
Ptolemy V Epiphanes   205–180
Ptolemy VI Philometor   180–145
Ptolemy VII Neos Philopator   145
Ptolemy VIII Euergetes II   170–116
Ptolemy IX Soter II   116–107
Ptolemy X Alexander I   107–88
Ptolemy IX Soter II (restored)   88–80
Ptolemy XI Alexander II   80
Ptolemy XII Neos Dionysus (Auletes)   80–51
Cleopatra VII Philopater   51–30
Ptolemy XIII   51–47
Ptolemy XIV   47–44
Ptolemy XV Caesarion   44–30

After the chronology in the British Museum Dictionary of Ancient Egypt *by Ian Shaw and Paul Nicholson*

Was the King Really Divine?

The belief in the divine nature of the position of pharaoh was central to the ideology of kingship in ancient Egypt. The term 'pharaoh' (*per-aa*) actually means 'great house' and it was not used to describe the ruler himself until the New Kingdom period (c.1550–c.1069 BC); before that time it was used to refer to the king's palace or the royal court.

The divinity of kingship was an important part of the Egyptian system of beliefs and social structure from the very beginning of the pharaonic period (c.3100 BC). Some very early inscriptions have been found that describe the king as *netjer* ('god') or, more usually, *nefer netjer* ('good god'), which may in fact indicate a lesser or minor god. Several inscriptions are also known in which the king is referred to as *aa netjer* ('great god').

▼ *Wings were a symbol of protection: Horus protected the king and the earth with his wings, as did the vulture mother and funerary goddesses.*

More is known about the ruler's identification with the god Horus: for example, that the falcon was a symbol of kingship from the Protodynastic Period. On the Narmer Palette, a falcon holds a rope in its talons which is attached to a ring through the nose of a semi-personified papyrus marsh. The falcon presumably symbolizes Narmer, whose victories are commemorated on this schist ceremonial palette, which was found in the 'Main Deposit' at Hierakonpolis and is now in the Cairo Museum.

Royal titles

From the Old Kingdom (c.2686–c.2181 BC), each king had five names, which were each introduced by an important title. Only one name was given to him at birth; the other four were bestowed when he was crowned king. They encapsulated the ideology of kingship. Two of the names were introduced by titles that stressed the rule of the king over two lands that had been united: 'He of the Sedge and the Bee' (*Nesw Bity*) and 'He of the Two Ladies' (*Nebty*) (see *The Concept of Duality*). The other two names – 'Horus' (*Hor*) and 'Golden Horus' (*Hor Nebw*) – could not have more clearly emphasized his identification with the god.

The office of kingship was decidedly male, and during the 3,000 or so years of pharaonic history female pharaohs were few and far between. The best known is probably Hatshepsut (c.1473–c.1458 BC), who necessarily had to make use of the masculine royal titles and regalia. She was even referred to as 'he' in the inscriptions on the walls of her mortuary temple at Deir el-Bahri on

▲ *In the Hypostyle Hall at Abydos the royal Horus image surmounts one of the king's titles, 'Mighty Bull', common during the New Kingdom.*

the west bank at Thebes. This is not to underestimate the political and religious importance of female members of the royal family – in particular the king's mother and wives (especially the 'Chief Royal Wife').

In the ruler's succession and coronation he re-created the myth (parts of which were recorded as early as the Pyramid Texts) of Horus rightfully ascending to the throne of his deceased father Osiris (see *The Death of Osiris* and *The Contendings of Horus and Seth*). On his accession the king was crowned with the Double Crown, which Horus is often depicted wearing in temple and tomb reliefs. The king would also have performed rituals identifying himself with the falcon god. Of particular significance would have been the symbolic triumph over the god Seth.

Festival of victory

Inscriptions and reliefs on the walls of the temple dedicated to Horus at Edfu describe the events of the annual Festival of Victory. Although these scenes date to the reign of Ptolemy IX (116–107 BC), rituals of this kind were probably being enacted as early as the New Kingdom (c.1550–c.1069 BC). The aim of the ritual drama was the annihilation of Seth. The king, identified as Horus, had to pierce Seth with ten harpoons. Seth took the form of a hippopotamus, and it is likely that a model hippopotamus would have been made for the festival; the final ritual certainly involved the eating of a cake in the shape of a hippopotamus. The act of harpooning this wild animal, whether symbolic or actual, was an ancient royal ritual that symbolized the triumph of order over the forces of chaos.

Royal regalia

At the front of his crown, the king wore the *uraeus*, the image of a rearing cobra poised ready to strike down any potential opponent of the ruler, and therefore any threat to the order of the state.

The royal insignia included various sceptres. Two of the most important were the 'crook' symbolising government and the flail, perhaps deriving from a fly whisk. The king might also be represented holding various weapons, such as the mace and the scimitar, to signify his role in the defence of order.

A false beard was another mark of royalty, tied under the chin by a cloth strap.

The king is also seen to play the part of Horus in the Ramesseum Dramatic Papyrus, which is now in the British Museum, London. This document dates to the reign of the Twelfth-Dynasty king Amenemhat III (c.1855–c.1808 BC), although the drama had originally been written down for the Jubilee Festival of king Senusret III (c.1874–c.1855 BC). The king, as Horus, had a conversation with the other gods; he received the 'Sacred Eye' (a powerful protective amulet); he ordered oxen to refrain from trampling on barley because it symbolized his father Osiris, the god of vegetation; and he engaged in mock battle with Seth.

It is clear that in such rituals the king was identified with Horus, but he was also believed to come under his protection. The magnificent diorite seated statue of the Fourth-Dynasty king Khafre (c.2558– c.2532 BC) has a beautifully sculpted Horus falcon on the back of the king's head, with the wings in a protective posture around it. In the Ramesside Period (c.1295–c.1069 BC), the figure of Horus became part of the royal headdress, with his outstretched wings wrapped around the crown.

Son of Re

In accordance with the mythology of kingship, the king's father (and thus by definition the deceased king) was identified with the god of the dead,

▲ *Seti I is depicted at Abydos wearing the Blue Crown* (Khepresh) *and burning incense before a seated deity.*

rebirth and vegetation, Osiris. But the divine parentage of the ruler differed according to the context. In the fivefold titles mentioned earlier, the king's birth name was introduced by the title 'Son of Re' (*Sa Re*) – that is, son of the sun god, whom the king was thought to join on his death. This title was first used by the Fourth-Dynasty king Djedefre (c.2566–c.2558 BC). The birth name (called the nomen) and the throne name (the prenomen), introduced by the titulary 'He of the Sedge and the Bee', were the two names that appeared in the royal cartouche (ancient Egyptian *shenu*). This oval outline represented an encircling rope with knotted ends, and was believed to have protective properties.

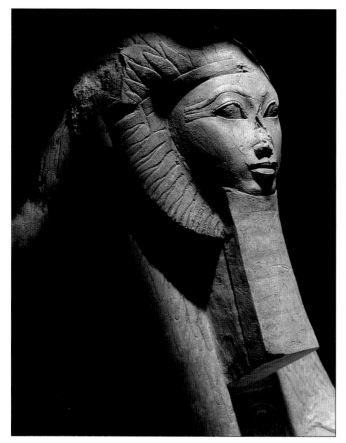

▲ *Hatshepsut, represented here as a sphinx, wore the false beard of the pharaoh despite the fact that she was a woman.*

In the New Kingdom Period (c.1550–c.1069 BC), rulers claimed to be the offspring of Amun, the 'king of the gods'. The 'divine births' of the Eighteenth-Dynasty rulers Hatshepsut (c.1473–c.1458 BC) and Amenhotep III (c.1390–c.1352 BC) were documented on the walls of Hatshepsut's mortuary temple at Deir el-Bahri and the temple of Luxor respectively (see *The Divine Birth of the Egyptian King*). These kings continued to use the title 'Son of Re', but this would not have appeared contradictory to the ancient Egyptians because Re, the supreme solar deity, had by this time been merged with Amun to become the principal deity Amun-Re.

A variety of religious texts show that the king might be identified with a range of deities, depending on the context. He was often referred to as being 'like' (*mi*) a particular god. A marvellous example of the comparisons made between a particular ruler and the divine world is the cycle of hymns composed in honour of the Twelfth-Dynasty king Senusret III (c.1874–c.1855 BC). The status accorded to kingship is exemplified by the occasional reference to the ruler as a creator god. For example, in the Twelfth-Dynasty tomb inscription of Khnumhotep at Beni Hasan, the king is referred to as Atum. In fact, throughout the Old Kingdom (c.2686–c.2181 BC), the king was said to have the divine powers of Sia (divine knowledge), Hu (divine utterance) and Heka (divine magic), which were usually attributed to the creator gods.

Inescapable mortality

In the eyes of the Egyptian people there must have been strict limitations on the living king's divinity, and clear distinctions were made in references to the king and the gods. During the Middle Kingdom (c.2055–c.1650 BC), the mortality of the man who held the divine office of king was acknowledged for the first time in some of the texts, such as *The Instruction of King Amenemhat I for his Son Senusret I*, the theme of which is regicide. Although written as if it were the advice of the Twelfth-Dynasty king Amenemhat I (c.1985–c.1955 BC) to his son and successor Senusret I (c.1965–c.1920 BC), it must have been composed during the latter's reign because it refers to the assassination of the older king. The tone of the piece is rational, personal and bitter, dealing as it does with the dangers of political office. The new king is warned about the treachery of his subjects in a manner that appears realistic and in conflict with the dogma of divine kingship.

The decision to emphasize the humanity as well as the divinity of the king can be seen in the art as well as the literature of this period. The statues of Senusret III (c.1874–c.1855 BC) and Amenemhat III (c.1855–c.1808 BC) of the Twelfth Dynasty, portray a sense of weariness in the faces, which are lined with age. These are a far cry from the typically stylized features of earlier Egyptian kings who, in representation, always had to appear youthful and vigorous. The fact that being pharaoh was a tough job was publicly acknowledged for the first time. In cases where the king was assassinated in a palace conspiracy, or if several kings died in quick succession, the mortality of the ruler would have been evident to all. Jubilee festivals were celebrated with the emphasis on the revivification of the king (see *Royal Jubilee Festivals*).

▼ *The large ears on this black granite statue of Senusret III might indicate the all-hearing capacity of the king. The more realistic royal portraiture of this era is also apparent.*

Glorification of the king

By the early New Kingdom (from c.1550 BC), the Old Kingdom (c.2686–c.2181 BC) was regarded as the glorious past, and the rulers emulated the heightened status of kingship of the Old Kingdom (whose pharaohs had certainly left their mark in the form of enormous pyramids). The king could be worshipped and supplicated for aid as a god. The Eighteenth-Dynasty king Akhenaten (c.1352–c.1336 BC) elevated himself and his family to the status of a divine royal family, whose members were then worshipped at shrines in households throughout his capital city of Akhetaten. The Nineteenth-Dynasty king Ramesses II (c.1279–c.1213 BC) built throughout Egypt on an incredible scale and covered the country with large images of himself, including four statues 21m (69ft) high fronting his temple at Abu Simbel in Lower Nubia, seemingly attesting to his divinity. He even had a cult worshipping him.

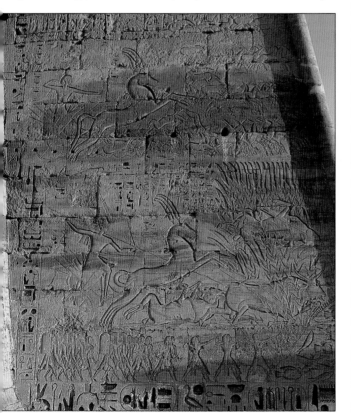

▼ *The wild bull hunt of Ramesses III, illustrated on the temple pylon at Medinet Habu, symbolized the king's control over chaos and potential danger to the Egyptian state. 20th Dynasty.*

Tutankhamun probably never went into battle but, as this decorated chest reveals, by his reign it had become standard practice to represent the king conquering his enemies, because the triumphant imagery had symbolic value.

The king as high priest

Throughout Egyptian history the pharaoh was nominally the high priest of every god in every temple throughout the country. (In practice high priests had to be appointed in each of the temples to function on behalf of the king.) In this way, the pharaoh stood as the intermediary between every god and the human world. Reliefs on the walls of the temples showed the king making offerings to the gods, and performing the required rituals before them. It was considered of prime importance that he should be portrayed as the one who presented *maat* (translated as 'truth', 'order' or 'justice') to the gods, because this was what the Egyptian gods lived on. It was the role of the king to ensure the beneficence of the gods and thereby ensure peace, harmony, and prosperity in Egypt. The king was essential to universal order, and it was his duty to maintain *maat* at all times. This function also involved quelling chaos, which was believed to manifest itself in wild animals and foreigners. Even if the king never actually involved himself in wild bull hunts and military campaigns abroad, the convention was for him to be depicted on temple walls engaged in such activities. In this way the king was symbolically subduing chaos and ensuring order. A common motif was the king smiting the enemy or a bound captive. It was essential for the dogma of divine kingship that the Egyptian ruler should always be portrayed as triumphant. The king's victories in battle were not, however, put down to the fact that he was a god, but that he had been granted them by the divine world, after the appropriate offerings and prayers.

It was traditional for a new pharaoh to have texts composed claiming that the land had been in a state of disorder prior to his ascent to the throne, and that, thanks to his greatness, he had restored it to its former balance and glory. Sometimes these texts did follow a period of upheaval, but they tend to be formulaic and together form a genre of literature that glorified the new king and legitimated his right to rule. ◆

The Divine Birth of the Egyptian King

The reliefs are fading fast in the colonnades of the west Theban mortuary temple at Deir el-Bahri, built in honour of the deceased Eighteenth-Dynasty ruler Hatshepsut (c.1473–c.1458 BC). But it is just possible to make out a series of scenes that tell an interesting story concerning ancient Egyptian ideas about kingship and their gods – the so-called 'divine birth' of their pharaoh.

Amun, the 'king of the gods' in the New Kingdom Period (c.1550–c.1069 BC), is shown being led by the hand to a queen's bedchamber by the ibis-headed Thoth, the 'messenger of the gods'. Amun is depicted in human form wearing the curled beard that was associated with divinity. He wears a tall, double-plumed headdress and holds a

▲ *The 'messenger of the gods' Thoth accompanies the 'king of the gods' Amun.*

was-sceptre (associated with divinity, power, well being and prosperity) in his free hand. The queen in question is Ahmose Nefertari, the wife of the Eighteenth-Dynasty king Tuthmosis I (c.1504–c.1492 BC).

The next scene is a wonderfully modest portrayal of the sexual union between the queen and Amun. They are shown fully dressed, seated upright together on a bed which is supported on the heads of two goddesses. Amun and the queen have their knees entwined and he holds an *ankh* (the sign of life) up to her nose: thus she takes in his vitality and procreative force.

Following this night of passion, in the next scene Amun passes on his instructions to Khnum, the ram-headed creator god. They both hold *was*-sceptres and *ankhs*. As a result of this meeting, Khnum fashions Ahmose Nefertari's

▼ *Amun, wearing the characteristic double-plumed headdress, is seated together with Queen Ahmose Nefertan in a euphemistic portrayal of sexual union.*

▼ *The goddess of childbirth, Heket attends the creation of Hatshepsut on Khnum's potter's wheel.*

daughter and the ruler-to-be, Hatshepsut, on his potter's wheel (see *Creation Myths*). Alongside the tiny figure of Hatshepsut on the wheel is an identical figure, representing her *ka* or 'spirit'. Heket, the frog-headed protective goddess of childbirth, is also present at this creation of the ruler.

Idealism in art

Ancient Egyptian art is highly stylized and idealized. Women are depicted as slender young beauties regardless of their actual age and looks, and it is almost unheard-of to find a representation of a pregnant woman. The scene of the pregnant queen being led to the birthing chamber by Khnum and Heket is one such rare example, although you have to look very closely to detect any sign of pregnancy – the queen's abdomen is only very slightly rounded. Like the sexual intercourse, the scene of the birth is entirely

euphemistic. A goddess, presumably acting as midwife, kneels before the seated queen and hands her the newborn child. Kneeling behind the queen is Meskhent, the goddess of the birthing bricks. Finally, Hatshepsut is presented before the gods, the most important of whom is of course her 'father', Amun.

Divine parentage

The idea of Amun being the father of the monarch was not particular to Hatshepsut, but as a woman, she might have felt it necessary to emphasize her legitimacy in this way. On the other hand she may well have felt no need for 'propaganda' of this kind, and in commissioning these reliefs she was merely doing what was expected of her as an Eighteenth-Dynasty ruler, emphasizing an aspect of the divinity of kingship.

Amenhotep III (c.1390– c.1352 BC) had a similar series of reliefs carved in the temple of Luxor on the east bank at Thebes. In this case the queen was Mutemwia, and although Amun was represented in his usual way (as at Deir el-Bahri), the

▲ *The queen's pregnancy is barely noticeable. She is accompanied by Khnum and Heket.*

hieroglyphs indicate that he took the guise of her husband Tuthmosis IV (c.1400–c.1390 BC) for the purpose of this ceremonial sexual union (perhaps to put the queen at ease).   ◆

▼ *Hatshepsut is presented before Amun, who holds an ankh in his right hand.*

Goddesses of childbirth

Women in ancient Egypt appear to have given birth in a crouching position supported on 'birthing bricks'. Because infant mortality was high and the Egyptians were well aware of the dangers of childbirth, they sought as much divine assistance and protection as possible, and the bricks were divinely personified as the deity Meskhent, one of the goddesses of fate who governed the future of newly born children.

The frog goddess Heket, at one time regarded as the consort of the creator god Khnum, acted as the divine midwife and was said to attend royal births. The protection of the hippopotamus goddess, Taweret, extended to all pregnant women.

Royal Jubilee Festivals

It was important for the king to remain strong and agile in the eyes of his people. This must have been very difficult if the king had been ruling for any length of time and had become noticeably stooped and wrinkly. The Sixth-Dynasty king Pepi II (c.2278–c.2184 BC), for example, supposedly reigned for around 94 years, so towards the end of his reign he can hardly have looked spry at public appearances.

It was traditional to celebrate a royal jubilee festival (*heb sed*) 30 years into the reign, but sometimes a king might choose to hold such a celebration at another time. Amenhotep III (c.1390–c.1352 BC), for example, is said to have ruled for 38 years and yet he celebrated three *heb seds*.

The festival consisted of a number of rituals which were intended to

▼ *This limestone fragment shows two figures of Akhenaten wearing the traditional short cloak of the* sed-*festival. On the right he is accompanied by his Chief Prophet, who carries the king's sandals. 18th Dynasty.*

rejuvenate the king, to display his fitness to continue ruling, to consolidate his claim to the land over which he ruled, and to ensure the fertility of the land. Reliefs depicting the events of such a festival emphasize the honouring of the enthroned king, who is often shown wearing a very particular short cloak and sitting in a pavilion special to the occasion. He is also depicted ceremonially running (often holding ritual implements) between markers which may well have symbolized the borders of Egypt, thereby staking his claim to the whole territory.

Royal athleticism

A very early depiction of a *sed*-festival can be seen on an ebony label in the British Museum, London. It was found at Abydos in the tomb of the First-Dynasty king Den (c.2950 BC). An illustration carved on the label shows Den wearing a Double Crown, sitting on his throne in a special festival pavilion. He is also shown running between two sets of three boundary markers – an

The Step Pyramid complex

It is still possible to visit the *heb sed* court to the south-east of Djoser's Step Pyramid. This open court is home to a number of 'dummy' shrines representing the ancient chapels of local gods of the nomes of Egypt. At its southern end is the base of what would originally have been a double festival pavilion containing two thrones, one to symbolize the king's rule over Upper Egypt, and the other to symbolize his rule over Lower Egypt.

image that crops up throughout pharaonic history.

The Third-Dynasty ruler Djoser (c.2667–c.2648 BC), for example, is portrayed running on a relief found in the underground chambers of his Step Pyramid complex at Saqqara. In fact various structures in this king's mortuary complex were dedicated to his

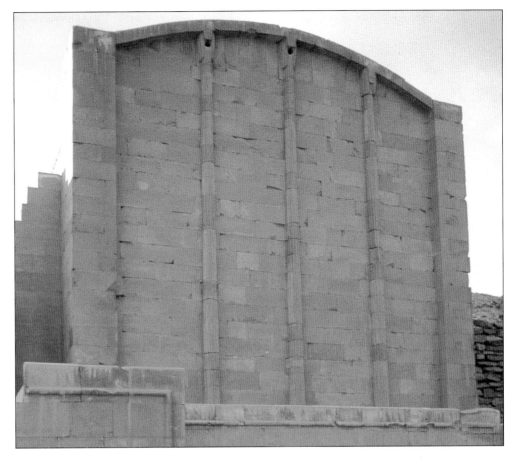

▶ *Dummy chapels such as this one were stone replicas of those built for the celebration of the sed-festival. Their presence in Djoser's Step Pyramid complex was intended to ensure that the king would be able to celebrate jubilee festivals throughout eternity. Old Kingdom.*

enactment of the *sed*-festival. The Step Pyramid does not stand alone, but is surrounded by a series of courts, temples, and other important buildings. In the large court to the south of the pyramid there are the traces of boundary markers, so perhaps this was where the king performed his ceremonial display of athleticism.

Commemorative buildings

Important religious buildings were still being built and decorated in connection with the royal jubilee festivals very much later in Egyptian history. Examples include the mortuary temple of the Eighteenth-Dynasty king Amenhotep III (c.1390–c.1352 BC) on the west bank at Thebes (of which only the two statues known as the Colossi of Memnon survive), as well as the temple to the Aten at east Karnak built by his successor Akhenaten (c.1352–c.1336 BC) and the *sed*-festival court at Bubastis built by the Twenty-second-Dynasty king Osorkon II (c.874–c.850 BC).

The large lake to the east of Amenhotep III's palace at Malkata on the west bank at Thebes appears to have been the setting for one of this king's splendid jubilee festivals, during which he was rowed in a boat in a ceremony reminiscent of the sun god's night-time journey through the Netherworld. The rejuvenation of the king reflected the rising of the sun (see *The Journey of the Sun through the Netherworld*). ◆

▶ *This false door stela in the South Tomb of Djoser's Step Pyramid Complex, shows the king performing the ceremonial* heb sed *run.*

Nearer to the Gods

The ancient Egyptians felt that they lived on earth under the protection of the gods, and believed that, so long as the gods were pleased by their worship and devotion, justice demanded that they would be given divine protection from war, famine and sickness.

Although their religion was dominated by a funerary cult, the Egyptians were not fearful of death. They saw it not as an end but as a brief interruption, and believed that life after death would proceed very much as before, preserving their social status, family connections, and even their physical belongings. Only those who failed to please the gods, or to prepare for death with the proper rituals, would be denied a continued existence. The deceased were judged, by Osiris and a tribunal of deities, to determine their fitness to proceed into the Afterlife.

Funerary rituals included mummification to preserve the physical body, which the Egyptians believed they would need after death as a vessel for their spirit, just as they would need all their possessions to make life comfortable. It was also important that their name was preserved and remembered, and funerary texts accompanied the deceased to protect them. These collections of spells and incantations were originally the prerogative of the pharaoh, but eventually became available to anyone who could afford to have them copied.

◀ *In royal mortuary temples built to honour the deceased kings, offerings were presented daily for the king's ka (spirit).*

Beliefs About the Afterlife

The preparations that accompanied burials from as early as Predynastic times (c.5500–c.3100 BC) reveal that the ancient Egyptians must have had beliefs about the existence of an Afterlife from very early on. These ideas were certainly formed well before the emergence of Pharaonic Egypt as we know it; that is, before the country was unified into an influential state with a sole ruler and an efficient, centralized government. Pre-dating any evidence for social stratification and the existence of a wealthy minority, there is evidence for burials involving the deposit of funerary goods in the grave alongside the body.

These items were not elaborate or specially crafted ceremonial artefacts, but basic objects of daily life, such as pots, tools and weapons. Presumably the people buried with these things believed that they would need them in a practical way after death. After all, a simple pot is unlikely to have been a token of sentiment or a prized possession; its presence in a tomb must have been considered functional.

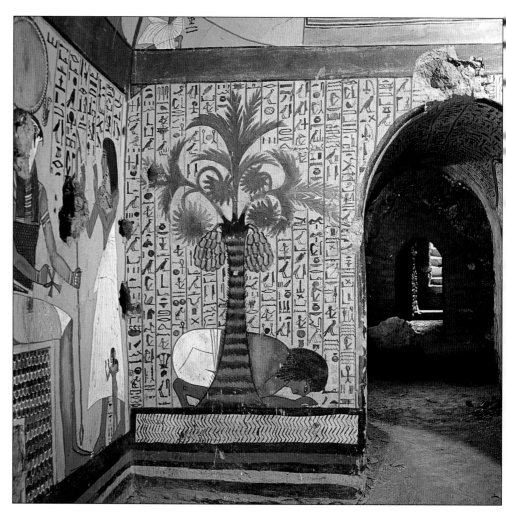

▼ *An Egyptian lady would have been buried with a selection of objects intended to ensure that she would be able to eat, adorn herself with jewellery, cosmetics and perfumed unguents, and perform rituals in the Afterlife. New Kingdom.*

▲ *In a land of extreme heat and vast desert expanses, a pool and the cool shade of a date palm were heavenly. By depicting them on the wall of his tomb, Pashedu hoped to enjoy their benefits in the Afterlife. 19th Dynasty. Thebes.*

Journeying into the Afterlife

The predynastic custom of burying dead bodies in the foetal position may suggest a belief in the concept of rebirth. Also, the accidental or deliberate unearthing of perfectly preserved bodies may have led the early Egyptians to believe that the dead were living on in some way. The emergence of the practice of mummification early in the Dynastic Period reveals the strongly held belief that the body was required to be intact for the Afterlife.

We can have no idea of what the ancient Egyptians imagined the Afterlife to be until they were able to write down a description of it. The funerary texts that were buried with the dead tell us that they ascended to the Afterlife and that it was located in the heavens – the realm of the sun. Several methods of ascent appear to have been possible. These included riding on the back of a falcon, goose or other bird; being wafted upwards with burning incense; climbing up a ladder formed by the outstretched arms of the gods; or travelling on a reed float or barque that was sailed, rowed or towed. The journey into the Afterlife was no mean feat – all manner of demons and other hazardous obstacles had to be bypassed and overcome. The funerary texts provided guidelines and directions for the routes to be taken, and certain spells and recitations to be uttered at the appropriate time.

Domains of the dead

The ancient Egyptians imagined the Afterlife as a perfect version of life as they knew it in the Nile Valley, with a constant superabundance of produce. The vignettes on papyrus that accompany the text in the Book of the Dead, and the scenes painted on the walls of non-royal tombs, also provide us with a picture of the Afterlife. They tend to show the tomb owner and his wife toiling in the fields, which they did not for one moment expect actually to do (or at least they hoped not to). They certainly would have taken precautions to safeguard against the possibility of any hard work.

▲ *The Book of the Dead includes illustrations of the final procession of the mummified body to the tomb and the last rites before burial, such as the Opening of the Mouth ceremony. The chain of events is depicted here on the papyrus of the high official Nebqed. New Kingdom.*

Egyptian paradise

The Egyptian paradise was called the Field of *Hetep* ('satisfaction' or 'offerings') – the land of Osiris, the god of the dead. The Coffin Texts (spells 464–468) and Chapter 110 of the Book of the Dead describe this land. It was associated with the western horizon (the place of the setting sun) and was imagined as a luscious place. Its fields were irrigated by channels full of water; its crops of emmer wheat, barley and flax grew tall and strong; its fruit trees were heavy with their loads of ripe dates and figs.

▶ *Sennedjem is depicted standing at the gate of the other world. A similar illustration was used to represent the vertical tomb shaft that separated the tomb chapel from the subterranean burial chamber below. 19th Dynasty. Thebes.*

The iconography of the ancient Egyptian religious belief system was strongly influenced by an underlying concept of duality – the importance of opposite but interdependent entities. The two horizons occurred frequently in both the solar and funerary aspects of the religion. Coupled with the Field of *Hetep*, which was associated with the western horizon, was the Field of *Iaru* ('reeds'), a place of purification that was associated with the eastern horizon, the site of the purification and 'rebirth' of the sun each dawn. Two other names that crop up in the funerary texts are '*Duat*' and '*Imhet*'. They were identified as separate locations in the sky: *Duat* referred to the eastern horizon, and *Imhet* to the western one. These terms might best be translated as 'Afterworld'. They are often rendered as 'Underworld' or 'Netherworld', but these translations can be misleading because the deceased appears to have ascended to them. Another name that came to be used as a general term for the Afterworld was *Rosetau* (literally, 'passage of dragging'). It originally referred to the sloping entranceway of a tomb; it was later used as the name for the necropolis of Memphis, and afterwards of Abydos.

Coming closer to the gods

The ancient Egyptians used strong visual images to illustrate, and even animate, their beliefs. The Afterworld was divinely personified as Aker. This was an earth divinity represented as a narrow tract of land with a human or lion head at each end, or sometimes in the form of two lions seated back to back, one facing east and one west (sometimes with the symbol for the horizon between them). These two creatures were thought to guard the entrance and exit to the Afterworld.

There is also evidence that the ancient Egyptians had a concept of an 'undersky' (*Nenet*) and an underworld where demons lived upside-down. As a result, because their mouths were where their anuses should have been, they had to eat their own faeces. Luckily, spells existed to avoid having to face what this place had to offer.

By dying and passing into the Afterlife, an individual was thought to become closer to the gods, and perhaps even influence the divine world. There is evidence to show that the dead were believed to possess supernatural powers that could solve various problems for the living. However, as well as proving helpful, the dead could cause serious disturbances for the living. The unsettled dead were often blamed for causing all kinds of distress, including illness. ◆

Ka, Ba and *Akh*

There are three important words which crop up repeatedly in the ancient Egyptian funerary texts, and which are variously translated as 'spirit' and 'soul'. It is probably best to leave them untranslated, because it is very difficult to be sure exactly what these terms meant to the ancient Egyptians, and a word such as 'soul' has connotations that would have been unfamiliar to them.

The hieroglyph used to write *ka* was a pair of arms, but in art the *ka* was represented as an individual's slightly smaller double. For example, in the 'divine birth' scenes on the walls of Hatshepsut's mortuary temple at Deir el-Bahri, two small and identical figures are depicted on a potter's wheel. These are the Eighteenth-Dynasty ruler Hatshepsut (c.1473–c.1458 BC) and her *ka* being created by the ram-headed creator god Khnum.

The *ka* was thought to come into being at the birth of an individual. Dying was sometimes described as 'joining one's *ka*'. The *ka* was intimately linked with the physical body, which was regarded

▼ *The* ba-*bird not only represented the concept of the 'soul', but also anonymous gods or powers, and as such was present on the walls of New Kingdom royal tombs.*

as the vessel for the *ka* after death. This explains the belief in the need for the survival of the body, and the measures taken to preserve it whenever possible. *Ka* is often translated as 'spirit' or 'vital force', as in the creative life force of an individual that enabled the generations to continue through the ages. It was believed that the *ka* required food and drink, so offerings were made to it for as long as possible after death. In fact the word *ka* sometimes means 'sustenance', depending on the context.

The hieroglyph used to write *ba* was a Jabiru stork, while in funerary art it was represented as a bird with a human head, and sometimes with human arms. The ancient Egyptian idea of the *ba* appears to have been similar to our concept of personality, that is the non-physical attributes that make any human being unique. It is possible that it also implied the moral essence of a person's motivation and movement. It was considered more mobile than the *ka* and it enabled the dead person to move about in the Afterlife. The ancient Egyptian word for 'ram' was also *ba*, and it was probably for this reason that the ram-headed deity Khnum was regarded as the *ba* of Re, the sun god.

The hieroglyph used to write *akh* was a crested ibis, although it was often portrayed as a *shabti*-like mummiform figure. It may well have been considered the result of the successful reunion at death of the *ba* and the *ka*, and it is sometimes translated as 'transfigured spirit'. Those who failed to achieve this transfiguration were condemned to eternal death.

Together with the *ka, ba,* and *akh*, two other important elements of a person's being, in both life and death, were their name and their shadow. It was believed vital to ensure that these two elements were remembered and protected after death in order that the deceased should survive in the Afterlife. ◆

▲ *Funerary statues were seen as images of the* ka *of the dead, and might incorporate the* ka *symbol on their head, as in the case of this statue of Awibre Hor.*

▼ *The crested ibis symbolizing the* akh *is distinguished by its characteristic ruff of head feathers. 19th Dynasty. Luxor.*

Pyramid Texts

The oldest surviving funerary texts – collections of spells or 'utterances' that accompanied a burial – are those known today as the Pyramid Texts. These were exclusively the prerogative of the king during the Old Kingdom and First Intermediate Period (c.2686–c.2055 BC). They dealt with his protection while he was still alive (particularly against dangerous animals), but were mainly concerned with his death and what was believed to happen to him afterwards. Later versions of funerary texts – known as the Coffin Texts and the Book of the Dead – were not confined to royal burials, and demonstrate the gradual democratization of funerary religion.

Written in hieroglyphs, the earliest appearance of the Pyramid Texts is as inscriptions on the inner walls of the corridors and chambers of the pyramid of Unas (c.2375– c.2345 BC), the last ruler of the Fifth Dynasty. It was built at Saqqara, one of the great cemeteries of the capital city of Memphis. A further eight pyramids of the Sixth Dynasty and early First Intermediate Period (c.2345–c.2125 BC) have been found to contain very similar inscriptions. Five of these pyramids belonged to kings, and the other three to wives of the Sixth-Dynasty ruler Pepi II (c.2278–c.2184 BC). The Pyramid Texts totalled some eight hundred spells, but no one pyramid was inscribed with all of them, the largest collection being the 675 texts found in the pyramid of Pepi II.

The funeral of the king

It has been suggested that the sequence of the spells relates to the funeral of the king, and the procession of his mummified body from the Valley Temple connected with his pyramid to his burial chamber within the pyramid. The king is identified with Osiris, the god of the dead and the Afterlife, and many of the spells in the burial chamber

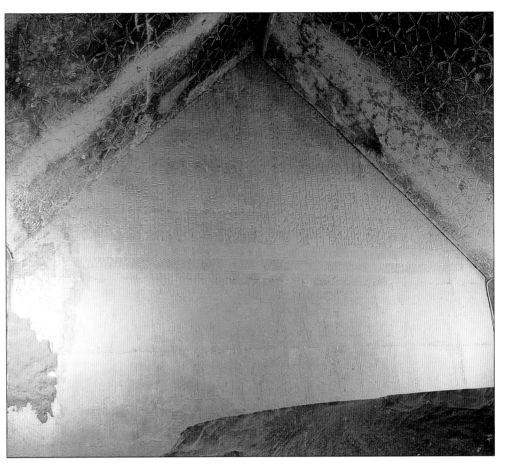

◀ By the 5th Dynasty the emphasis was no longer on enormous grandeur but on the hieroglyphic inscriptions within pyramids such as that of Teti, and the reliefs on the walls of the associated mortuary temples. Saqqara.

would probably have been recited by the Lector Priest at the funeral. The earliest known recording of the Opening of the Mouth ceremony and early offering rituals are to be found in these texts. The purpose of many of the spells was to protect the dead king in the Afterlife. Because the language in which they are written is archaic in places, it is likely that these were in fact very ancient spells, recorded for the first time in the Old Kingdom.

The emphasis on the cult of the sun god in the texts implies that perhaps they were composed by the priests at Heliopolis, the cult centre of Re. This temple and its priesthood had had close associations with the king since at least the Fourth Dynasty. Utterance 264 is one of many spells that refer to the king's ascension to the realm of the sun. It ends:

The Nurse Canal is opened, the Winding Waterway is flooded, the Fields of Reeds are filled with water, so that the king is ferried over on it to that eastern side of the sky, to the place where the gods fashion him, where he is born again new and young.

The idea was that when the king died he went to join the sun god on his journey through the sky by day and the Netherworld by night. This journey was thought to be made by boat, and it was believed that when the sun god reached

◀ The behaviour attributed to Nut of swallowing and giving birth to the sun – depicted here in Ramesses IX's burial chamber – was ultimately an enigma, as indicated by her epithet shetayit, *which means 'mysterious one'.*

the eastern horizon, just before dawn, he was purified in Nun, the waters of creation. The rising of the sun was identified with the dead king's rebirth.

Rebirth of the king

It has been suggested that names such as the 'Nurse Canal', 'Winding Waterway' and 'Field of Reeds' found in the Pyramid Texts refer to parts of the sky goddess Nut's anatomy. One mythological explanation as to where the sun went at night described it as being swallowed by the sky goddess in the evening, and being given birth to by her at dawn. Nut was often depicted on the ceiling of burial chambers and inside the lid of sarcophagi, displaying the idea that the dead person, like the sun, would be reborn. It may be that, in the Pyramid Texts, the idea of the dead king passing through the body of the goddess is being expressed in metaphorical terms.

The imperishable stars

The Pyramid Texts imply that the king was believed to join the circumpolar stars in the northern sky – the 'imperishable stars' that never disappear

▲ The ceiling of the burial chamber in the pyramid of Teti is a vault of stars. The Pyramid Texts are inscribed in columns of hieroglyphs on the chamber walls.

from view. In this way these early royal funerary texts equate the dead king with Osiris, the sun and the stars. They also include hymns to the gods and a long list of offerings of food, drink and clothing. These were to be made at the time of the burial and renewed after the king's death, ideally for eternity, because it was believed that they would sustain the king in the Afterlife. ◆

Fifth-Dynasty pyramids

Instead of the solid limestone blocks used for the great monuments erected during the Fourth Dynasty, the pyramids of the Fifth Dynasty were built from small, roughly-dressed stones, but the inner decoration of their burial chambers and funerary complexes was more lavish than ever before.

Coffin Texts

By the Middle Kingdom (c.2055 BC), it was not only kings and queens who were thought to benefit from having funerary texts included in their burials, but also members of the administrative élite. This fortunate minority was not buried in pyramids but in rock-cut tombs. The spells to aid their transition into the Afterlife were recorded in cursive hieroglyphs on the interior walls of their wooden coffins. This accounts for the

▼ *Vignettes in the* Book of Two Ways *show that features of the waterway and landway were guarded by demons brandishing knives. This coffin belonged to Gua, Chief of Physicians. 12th Dynasty.*

origin of the modern term 'Coffin Texts' – although they have also been found on tomb walls, sarcophagi, statues and stelae in offering chapels.

The Book of Two Ways

More than 1,000 Coffin Texts have been collected. They are derived from the body of royal funerary texts known as the Pyramid Texts, with some careful editing and important additions. The chief component of the Coffin Texts is a detailed guidebook to the Afterlife, known as the *Book of Two Ways*. It has been found drawn inside the bottoms of wooden coffins discovered at el-Bersher, the cemetery of Hermopolis Magna, and the cult centre of Thoth, the lunar deity

of scribes and wisdom. The occupant of the coffin was promised an Afterlife like that of the deceased king, and the chance to travel in the sun god's solar barque. But there was a condition: he had to be able to reel off the right spells and a brief rendition of the theology of the sun god Re. At the end of the *Book of Two Ways* we find the pledge:

As for any person who knows this spell, he will be like Re in the east of the sky, like Osiris in the midst of Duat.

Like the king in the Pyramid Texts, the dead person was assured that he would be reborn into the Afterlife, just as the sun rose at dawn above the eastern horizon, and he would become one not only with the sun god but also with Osiris, god of the dead. It would have been a useful *aide-mémoire* for the deceased to have the words of the spells (which he was expected to know by heart) written on the inside of his coffin.

Map of the Afterlife

There are two versions of the *Book of Two Ways*, and both are thought to have been composed at Hermopolis Magna. Both include references to the non-royal deceased becoming stars in the sky, alongside Thoth. The Coffin Texts were accompanied by the earliest known map of the Afterlife, and on it the Mansion of Thoth is located in the Place of Maat. This map was specifically designed to guide the spirit of the deceased on its journey into the Afterlife. Knowledge of the spells and possession of the map meant that the deceased might become an *akh aper* ('equipped spirit').

The map located the Mansion of Osiris and the Field of *Hetep* (the Egyptian paradise), where the deceased might continue to serve Osiris. However, as in the Pyramid Texts, the Heliopolitan influence is unmistakable because the largest part of the plan indicated the path followed by the sun god on his voyage. First it moved from east to west along a blue waterway through the inner sky, then it went back again from west to east on a black landway through the outer sky. As in the myth of *The Journey of the Sun through the Netherworld*, found on the walls of royal tombs in the Valley of the Kings dating from the New Kingdom (c.1550–c.1069 BC), the Coffin Texts described the path of the sun god (and thus the deceased) as beset by demons, often wielding knives, throw sticks, spears or nets. If trapped by a demon, it was believed that the dead person might be beheaded, hacked to pieces or burned to death. The most dangerous was the giant serpent Apophis, who threatened to devour the sun every day before dawn, and so had to be symbolically destroyed by the sun's entourage every 24 hours. The only way for the spirit of the deceased to safely pass these obstacles (and others such as mounds, rivers, and gates of fire) was by learning their names and characteristics beforehand. ◆

▲ *Eyes painted on the coffin wall allowed the deceased to see out. Middle Kingdom.*

◀ *The inner coffin of the Commander Sepi is painted with a false door beneath the eyes.* Middle Kingdom.

Seeing eyes

Rectangular coffins of the Middle Kingdom were oriented in the tomb with the head to the north. Eyes were painted on the side of the coffin so that the mummy, whose face was positioned behind them, could see out. The body was therefore laid on its left side, facing east towards the rising sun.

Often the eyes were painted above a niched palace façade (*serekh*) design, or a false door, through which the spirit could pass in and out of the coffin.

The Book of the Dead

The end of the Second Intermediate Period (c.1550 BC) witnessed still further democratization of the Afterlife (see *Coffin Texts*), with the emergence of a collection of nearly 200 spells (or chapters). Today these are known as the Book of the Dead, but they were known to the ancient Egyptians as the '*Formulae for Going Forth by Day*'. These funerary texts came to accompany more people to the grave than ever did the Pyramid Texts (a purely royal prerogative) or Coffin Texts, since they were available to anyone who could afford to have them copied. The text was in fact an edited and supplemented version of the Coffin Texts (as the Coffin Texts had been of the Pyramid Texts), which continued to be included in the burials of wealthy people well into the Graeco-Roman Period (332 BC–AD 395).

Although there were 200 or so spells altogether, each burial contained only as many as the deceased or his family chose (or could afford) to have copied. They have mainly been discovered written on papyrus rolls, although certain spells have also been found recorded on coffins, amulets (such as Chapter 30A inscribed on heart scarabs, tomb walls, figurines (for example Chapter 6 on *shabtis*) and statuary.

The papyrus rolls were often placed in the coffin alongside the body, or they might be wrapped up in the mummy bandaging or inserted into a hollowed-out statuette of Ptah-Sokar-Osiris, the Memphite funerary deity, which was then deposited in the tomb along with a range of other funerary goods. These funerary texts were usually written in hieroglyphs, but Books of the Dead in the more cursive scripts, hieratic and demotic, have also survived. The texts were usually accompanied by brightly coloured illustrations or vignettes, ranging from depictions of the amulets to be included in the mummy wrappings to detailed scenes of the Afterlife.

The form of the book

No one copy of the Book of the Dead contained all the spells that were available, although by the Late Period the sequence had become relatively fixed. Egyptologists refer to the spells as numbered 'chapters', following the system imposed in 1842 by Karl Richard Lepsius (1810–84), when he edited the text of the Book of the Dead of Iufankh from the Ptolemaic Period. This example contained 165 chapters. The most significant texts, such as that concerned with the Weighing of the Heart ceremony, were the most lavishly illustrated.

Towards the end of the Ptolemaic Period, the funerary texts grew shorter and the Book of the Dead tended to be replaced by the Book for Breathing or the Book for Out-lasting Eternity. These short compositions could be written on single sheets, to be placed at the head and feet of the deceased. They still provided safeguards for his or her passage into the Afterlife, such as the requisite denial of short-comings for the deceased to present at the Weighing of the Heart ceremony.

▶ *This painted wooden* shabti *from the tomb of Ramesses IV is equipped with a hoe in each hand ready to break up heavy soil in the Afterlife on behalf of the deceased king. 20th Dynasty.*

◄ *In the funerary and other religious texts, it is rare to find lines or columns of writing without illustrations alongside. Vignettes tend to accompany the spells throughout the Book of the Dead. These spells in Kahapa's Book of the Dead are written in hieratic, a cursive form of hieroglyphs. Late Period.*

Becoming Osiris

Like the Pyramid Texts of the Old Kingdom (c.2686–c.2181 BC) and the Coffin Texts of the Middle Kingdom (c.2055–c.1650 BC), the main purpose of the Book of the Dead was to provide the deceased person with a collection of spells that would ensure his or her safe passage into the Afterlife. But, unlike the earlier texts, the spells included in the Book of the Dead were dominated by the cult of Osiris, the god of the dead and the Afterlife, rather than that of the sun god Re. Dead people came to be referred to as Osiris, and identification with this god was clearly considered to be the desired goal. It was also Osiris who sat in supreme judgment over the dead, determining their fitness for acceptance into the Afterlife.

Amulets and demons

The texts and their accompanying illustrations provide information on where and when amulets or papyri were to be placed on the body during embalming. Some objects were to be wrapped up in the bandaging, others were to be only temporarily brought into contact with the body. The texts also convey an idea of how the ancient Egyptians imagined the Afterlife they hoped to enter (see *Beliefs about the Afterlife*). As recorded in the Coffin Texts, there were a whole host of threatening demons and other obstacles that stood between the deceased and his or her arrival in 'paradise'. Probably the most crucial section of the Book of the Dead was Chapter 125, which described the final judgment of the dead person before Osiris. His or her lifetime was assessed to check that he or she had behaved well enough to be reborn into the Afterlife. If an ancient Egyptian could afford the inclusion of only one chapter of the Book of the Dead in the burial, he or she would have been well advised to choose this one.

► *By the Middle Kingdom, Sokar had been syncretized with the gods Ptah and Osiris, and prayers were being addressed to him as a funerary deity. Here, he is accompanied by the Horus falcon. Ptolemaic Period.*

Wherever possible, Egyptians took as many precautions as they could to ensure the comfort of their spirits after death (and who would blame them?). Just one example of this, from an incredible variety of spells, is Chapter 162, the purpose of which was to ensure that the deceased would be kept warm in the next life. ◆

Mythologizing Ancient Egypt

Outsiders have always regarded Egypt as an alien place. Its monuments have inspired awe, and the customs of its people have aroused fascination. The civilization of Pharaonic Egypt is so remote that although much evidence has been unearthed we still know relatively little – the scope for misinterpreting or even inventing Egypt's past is huge.

Until the early nineteenth century scientific archaeology was not practised and hieroglyphic script had not been deciphered, so the ancient texts were unfathomable. It is easy to see how 'Egypt of the Pharaohs' came to be mythologized. Scholars of the Western world based their understanding of ancient Egypt on the works of the classical writers, but we now know that these are far from reliable. The Graeco-Roman perception of Egypt was largely created from the legendary poems of Homer and the often inaccurate writings of Herodotus.

Despite great advances in archaeology and philology, the modern age continues to mythologize Egypt's past. Hollywood has helped to foster absurd ideas such as the 'curse of the mummy', and followers of the New Age movement have looked to Egypt as a fount of mysterious knowledge. ◆

◀ *The Great Sphinx, guardian of Khafre's valley temple, has intrigued travellers to Egypt over the centuries. Illustration from* Views in Egypt *by Luigi Mayer (1801)*

The Legacy of the Classical Writers

Until the early nineteenth century, the West's understanding (or misunderstanding) of ancient Egypt had much to do with the works of classical authors, although the seventeenth century did see the first 'archaeological' visits to Egypt. Men such as the English astronomer John Greaves (1602–52) visited Giza twice, measured and examined the pyramids, made a critical analysis of the classical writings about them, and published *Pyramidographia, or a Discourse on the Pyramids in Aegyt* in 1646. Another was the Frenchman Claude Sicard (1677–1726), who visited Upper Egypt four times and was the first modern traveller to identify the sites of Thebes and to

◀ *Serapis was a Ptolemaic invention: a combination of the Egyptian gods Osiris and Apis, represented as a Hellenistic deity (his attributes were those of Zeus, Helios, Hades, Asklepios and Dionysos). Marble sculpture from Pergamon, 2nd century AD.*

▲ *Herodotus was quite clearly mistaken when he wrote, '...they [the Egyptians] have no need to plough or hoe, or to use any other ordinary methods of cultivating their land.' A wall painting from the tomb of Sennedjem shows him farming with his wife. 18th Dynasty.*

ascribe correctly the Colossi of Memnon and the Valley of the Kings on the basis of classical descriptions.

The father of history

The greatest influence on the classical writers who documented Egypt was Herodotus (c.490–c.420 BC), who is often referred to as the 'Father of History'. He was certainly the best-known tourist in classical times. He was born in Halicarnassus in Caria on the south-western coast of Asia Minor. He wrote a series of nine books called *The Histories*, whose purpose was to trace the events that brought Greece into conflict with Persia. Within this framework, he also recorded all the

information he had been able to collect – and he was undoubtedly an avid collector of information.

Herodotus was probably in Egypt some time between 450 and 430 BC, and it is Book II of his series that describes Egypt. He appears to have gone to some length to collect information in Memphis, which he then sought to have backed up in Thebes and Heliopolis. Wisely, he spoke to priests, who were educated and had access to the nation's archives housed in the temples. But he relied wholly on oral testimony, and he was not familiar with the Egyptian language. He may have misunderstood much of what he was told and, as a foreigner, the Egyptian priests are unlikely to have disclosed much information to him. Quite clearly he did not believe all that he was told, but he chose to record it nonetheless, thereby ensuring the propagation of bizarre stories about ancient Egypt, both via an oral tradition and a written one. For example, after recounting a tale of a phoenix which was said to fly from Arabia to Heliopolis every 500 years, with his dead father in an egg of myrrh, he added, 'I give the story as it was told me...but I don't believe it.'

Herodotus was particularly interested in religion, medicine, mummification, customs and taboos, architecture (especially that of the pyramids) and astronomy; as well as geography (especially the flooding of the Nile), transport, flora, fauna, food, clothing, and historical events. He was intrigued by what he learnt, and had great respect for the country and its people:

About Egypt I shall have a great deal more to relate because of the number of remarkable things the country contains, and because of the fact that more monuments which beggar description are to be found there than anywhere else in the world.

▼ *The Palestrina Mosaic formed part of a floor in the Italian town of Praeneste (Palestrina). It probably dates to the early 1st century BC and its subject is a Nilotic landscape, showing the popularity of Egyptian themes in the Roman world.*

▲ *The Rosetta Stone records in Greek, demotic and hieroglyphic scripts the religious ceremonies attending the coronation of Ptolemy V in 205 BC.*

Herodotus felt that he was in a position to compare Egypt with other parts of the ancient world, and the Egyptian people with their neighbours. Because of the stable climate, for example, he wrote, '...next to the Libyans, they are the healthiest people in the world'.

He attempted to explain the inundation of the River Nile, and supplied various theories, such as the occurrence of seasonal winds that checked the flow of the river current towards the sea; the melting of snow in the southern mountains; and the supernatural nature of the river. His own explanation was elaborate, involving the sun, evaporation and winds dispersing the vapours, but the cause of the annual flood was basically deemed a mystery.

Unwittingly, Herodotus laid the foundations for a confused picture of life in Pharaonic Egypt. He wrote:

...the Egyptians themselves in their manners and customs seem to have reversed the ordinary practices of mankind.

He recorded, for instance, that women traded at market while men stayed at home and wove; that women urinated standing up and men sitting down; that they kneaded dough with their feet and clay (and even dung) with their hands. He was fascinated by the Egyptians' relationship with animals, especially the keeping and mummification of sacred animals. His description of their obsession with cats was particularly unreliable:

What happens when a house catches fire is most extraordinary: nobody takes the least trouble to put it out, for it is only the cats that matter: everyone stands in a row, a little distance from his neighbour, trying to protect the cats, which nevertheless slip through the line, or jump over it, and hurl themselves into the flames. This causes the Egyptians deep distress.

▶ *Egyptian scribes wrote using a rush brush. The Greeks introduced reed pens, which were adopted by the Egyptians by the 1st century AD. 25th Dynasty.*

Herodotus's writings on the actual history of Egypt are confused and his chronology is very jumbled. Even for Herodotus, writing in the fifth century BC, the beginnings of Dynastic Egypt were shrouded in the distant past, and the pyramids were already ancient and mysterious tourist attractions. He was, however, in a position to provide relatively accurate information concerning the Twenty-sixth Dynasty (664–525 BC), and the invasion of Egypt by the Persian ruler Cambyses in 525 BC.

Diodorus Siculus

Both the historian Diodorus Siculus (c.40 BC) and the historian and geographer Strabo (c.63 BC–c.AD 24) imitated Herodotus. Diodorus Siculus was born in Agyrium in Sicily. He visited Egypt between c.60 and 56 BC, and described Egypt in the first book of his *Bibliotheca Historica*, which set out to cover the history of the world up to Julius Caesar's conquest of Gaul. He was clearly amazed by some of the customs he believed to be typically Egyptian and, like Herodotus, he included among these

▲ *By the age of 17, Champollion had already learnt to read Arabic, Syrian, Chaldean, Coptic, Latin, Greek, Sanscrit and Persian. Portrait by Léon Cogniet, 1831.*

Champollion

The ancient Egyptian written sources were unintelligible until Jean François Champollion le Jeune (1790–1832) deciphered hieroglyphs. Working on the replicated hieroglyphic and Greek inscriptions on the Rosetta Stone (a priestly decree issued in 196 BC inscribed on a slab of black granite, now in the British Museum), he just beat the English scholar Thomas Young with the publication of his findings in 1822, though he did not achieve his ambition of visiting Egypt until 1828.

Using his knowledge of Coptic, Champollion was able to deduce not only the meaning of hieroglyphs and hieratic text but the structure of ancient Egyptian grammar.

mummification and the excessive treatment and worship of animals. He related the revenge of an Alexandrian mob on a Roman ambassador who had accidentally killed a cat (there is no ancient Egyptian evidence for this kind of behaviour). The pyramids and the Nile also fascinated him.

Strabo
Born in Pontus in north-eastern Asia Minor, Strabo spent several years in Alexandria in about 27 BC, and discussed Egypt in the eighth book of his *Geography*, published in c.23 AD.

His descriptions include those of Alexandria, the Faiyum, Theban monuments such as the Colossi of Memnon and the Valley of the Kings, and the Nilometer at Elephantine.

Strabo travelled with the Roman Prefect Aelius Gallus, escorted by priests and guides. In the seventeenth book of *Geography* he claims that tourists continued to be fascinated by the Nile, the monuments, the religion and the funerary customs, the exotic animals and worship of them, and the superior wisdom of the priests. One of his aims seems to have been to verify whether the sites of Egypt were worthy of their reputations. He decided that the following were: the oases; the tombs in the Valley of the Kings; the boating stunts at Philae; the pyramids; and the

stone chips around the pyramids, said to be petrified beans that were eaten by the pyramid builders.

Misinterpreting hieroglyphs
None of the classical writers appears to have made any effort to understand hieroglyphs, and until they were deciphered in the early nineteenth century, they tended to be regarded as esoteric and magical. The Renaissance in Europe heralded a keen interest in ancient Egypt, and one of the first classical texts to resurface and be studied in the fifteenth century was Horapollo's *Hieroglyphica*, dating to the fourth century AD. Rather than the true meaning of the ancient inscriptions, this gave symbolic explanations of hieroglyphs, which were believed to encapsulate profound truths.

In the seventeenth century, the Jesuit scholar Athanasius Kircher (1601–1680) published several volumes of entirely fictitious interpretations of hieroglyphic inscriptions, reflecting the theory that hieroglyphic signs were mystical symbols, which could be used to explain the secrets of the Egyptian cosmos. ◆

Misunderstanding the Pyramids

The breathtakingly enormous size of some of the pyramids, their immense antiquity and the fact that it is impossible to know with certainty how they were built (because no texts have been discovered to inform us), have resulted in some wild, unfounded speculation about them. It was Herodotus who first established the mistaken association between the construction of the Great Pyramid and the employment of slave labour, with no mention made of the corvée system. He also propagated the story that Khufu had forced his daughter to prostitute herself in return for blocks of stone, which were then used to build the middle of the three queens' pyramids to the east of the Great Pyramid.

In the first century AD the slave labour myth was augmented by the Jewish historian Josephus, who stated that the Hebrews were worn out during their sojourn in Egypt by, among other great toils, being forced to build pyramids. In fact the pyramids at Giza were constructed over a millennium before the time of the Hebrews.

Building the pyramids

We still do not know exactly how the Pyramids were built. Theories vary, but often include artificial flooding to provide a level, and the construction of earth ramps up which to drag the stone blocks. The enormous labour force needed to erect the pyramids and other great Egyptian monuments was assembled under a regime of obligatory service to the state, known as the corvée system. Each household had to provide food supplies or manpower for the state building projects. An advantage of becoming a priest was the chance of exemption from this conscription.

Arab legends

When the Arabs conquered Egypt in AD 642, they clearly marvelled at the pyramids and were quick to mythologize them. One popular Arab legend claimed that the great pyramid at Giza was in fact the tomb of Hermes (the Greek deity identified with the Egyptian god of wisdom and the scribal profession, Thoth). The purpose of the pyramid was said to be to conceal the literature and science held within it, well hidden from the eyes of the uninitiated, and to protect them from the flood – seemingly a merging of the catastrophic Biblical flood and the annual inundation of the River Nile. If we were to believe the Yemeni Arabs, the pyramids of Khufu and Khafre on the Giza plateau were actually the tombs of their ancient kings, one of whom was said to have defeated the Egyptians.

According to an early Coptic legend, a certain King Surid was responsible for the construction of the three pyramids at Giza. It tells that he had scientific knowledge recorded on their internal walls; sculptures and treasure placed inside them; and an idol positioned

▲ Europeans were fascinated by pyramids, which they tended to represent with impossibly steep sides. This scene is from a peepshow box of c.1750 depicting the Seven Wonders of the World.

outside each of the pyramids to guard it. Surid was said to have been buried in the 'Eastern Pyramid' (Khufu's), his brother Hujib in the 'Western Pyramid' (Khafre's), and Hujib's son Karuras in the 'Pied Pyramid' (Menkaure's).

Continuing this tradition, the fifteenth-century Arab historian al-Maqrizi recorded that an ancient king named Surid decorated the walls and ceilings of his pyramid chambers with scientific imagery and depictions of stars and planets. He was also supposed to have filled the chambers with hordes of treasure, including miraculous iron weapons that would never rust and glass that could bend without breaking. Al-Maqrizi also stated that when King Surid died, he was buried in the pyramid together with all his possessions. It is possible that the name Surid was a corruption of 'Suphis', the name used by Herodotus in the fifth century BC when referring to Khufu.

The story of the tremendous treasure buried inside the Great Pyramid can also be found in the tale of *The Thousand and One Nights* (also known as *The Arabian Nights*), along with the description of what is said to be the first ever break-in to the pyramid, in about AD 820, by Caliph al-Mamun, the son of Haroun al-Rashid. His men are said to have used iron picks and crowbars, and to have heated the stones with fire and then poured cold vinegar on them. It is, in fact, highly likely that the first forced entry into the Great Pyramid took place in antiquity, and that al-Mamun's men made use of a passage created by ancient thieves. A man named Denys of Telmahre, the Jacobite Patriarch of Antioch, was present when al-Mamun entered the pyramid, and he states that the pyramid had already been opened before their visit. This particular tale of the alleged earliest break-in was indeed rather too fanciful to be true. The same (albeit tamed) story was recorded by Abu Szalt of Spain. Rather than fabulous treasure, he reports that al-Mamun's men discovered only a sarcophagus with some old bones inside it.

Joseph's granaries

The Coptic and Arab myths were certainly closer to the truth than the explanations of medieval Europeans. Pilgrims to the Holy Land also chose to visit Egypt in order to see sites such as the pyramids, which they believed to be

▶ *The Freemasons adopted religious imagery for their secret rites, as shown by this nineteenth century Italian design for a Masonic temple. 19th century.*

the 'granaries of Joseph' (an idea recorded as early as the fifth century AD in the Latin writings of Julius Honorius and Rufinus). The pyramids were also depicted as granaries in, for example, a mosaic dating to the twelfth century in one of the domes of St Mark's in Venice. Many later fifteenth- and sixteenth-century representations of pyramids were just as inaccurate, even when

▲ *The new entrance to the Louvre Museum in Paris is a high-tech glass pyramid.*

executed by people who had actually seen them. They tended to be portrayed with much steeper sides than the real things, thereby mirroring more familiar classical monuments.

Mysteries of the pyramids

The seventeenth century saw the advocating, especially by Athanasius Kircher, of the magical and mystical significance of the pyramids - a belief still held by many people today. Modern theories about the pyramids range from the downright silly, such as their construction by aliens, to the less absurd, such as their alignment with the belt of Orion. The weird and wonderful connections made with the pyramids are endless, including their power to achieve immortality and world peace. Even if the ancient pharaohs had not intended any of these associations, they would no doubt be extremely satisfied to find that their pyramids are still inspiring awe and wonder in the twenty-first century AD. ◆

The Curse of the Pharaohs

Everyone loves a good story. Everyone also loves to be scared witless when they can maintain a safe and comfortable distance from the object of their fear. 'Strange and mysterious Egypt', with its dark tombs and ancient mummies, is the perfect setting for terror and intrigue. It is hardly surprising, therefore, that Hollywood was quick to capitalize on the 'Curse of the Mummy'. This idea was, in fact, a popular theme in literature from the mid-nineteenth century onwards. Authors such as Bram Stoker and Arthur Conan Doyle were keen to write about the awful revenge wrought by mummies whose tombs had been disturbed.

Tutankhamun's tomb

It was the discovery of the almost intact tomb of the Eighteenth-Dynasty ruler Tutankhamun (c.1336–c.1327 BC) that

▼ *Tutankhamun's mummy lay in a close-fitting nest of three anthropoid coffins (the innermost of solid gold) inside a quartzite sarcophagus.*

▲ *Two life-sized black wooden statues of the king guarded the entrance to his burial chamber, seen here just after the door seal had been broken.*

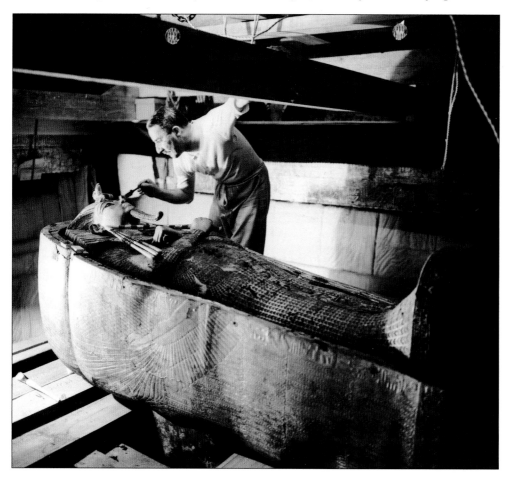

resulted in worldwide Egyptomania and an obsession with the ancient curse of the pharaohs. The great discovery was made by the archaeologist Howard Carter (1874–1939) while excavating in the Valley of the Kings, in the employment of the fifth Earl of Carnarvon. On 4th November 1922 he discovered a flight of steps leading down to a blocked door covered in seals bearing the cartouche of Tutankhamun. On entering the tomb on 26th November, 'the day of days', it was found to contain the body of the boy-king and the most incredible quantity of marvellous funerary goods.

Not only was this a discovery of breathtaking gold treasure, but its owner Tutankhamun had been buried in an unusual tomb. He had died in his teens, and he was closely connected with the infamous King Akhenaten (c.1352–c.1336 BC), who had made revolutionary changes to the art and religion of Egypt. People's imaginations began to run wild.

Within six months, on 5th April 1923,

▲ *Before removing the contents of Tutankhamun's tomb to Cairo, every object had to be scientifically recorded, photographed and often conserved. The king's body was left in his tomb, inside his outer coffin in the sarcophagus.*

Lord Carnarvon died, and in newspapers around the world his unexpected death was instantly blamed on 'the curse'. Conan Doyle declared that it was the result of 'elementals – not souls, not spirits – created by Tutankhamun's priests to guard the tomb'. One newspaper printed the translation of a curse said to be written in hieroglyphs on the door of the second shrine: 'They who enter this sacred tomb shall swift be visited by wings of death.' But this curse was wholly fictitious, as were all the other curses reported to the press, such as the one said by a necromancer to have been found by Carter carved in hieroglyphs on a stone at the entrance of the tomb. It was supposed to have read: 'Let the hand raised against my form be withered! Let them be destroyed who attack my name, my foundation, my effigies, the images like unto me!'

Carnarvon had been a weak man ever since a car accident, and was exhausted by the circumstances surrounding the discovery of Tutankhamun's tomb. He accidentally cut open a mosquito bite while shaving; it became infected, and he ended up with a fever. In this further weakened state, he fell prey to pneumonia. Some of the newspapers suggested that Carnarvon had pricked himself while in the tomb on a sharp object, such as an arrowhead, doctored with a poison so potent that it was still active after 3,000 years. Other articles in the press reported that Carnarvon had become infected by deadly micro-organisms that had laid dormant for millennia.

Rumours spread like wildfire. It was said that at the moment of his death, all the lights went out in Cairo, and his son and heir, Lord Porchester, sixth Earl of Carnarvon, claimed that at their family home in Highclere Castle in England his father's favourite dog howled and dropped down dead at exactly the same moment as the earl passed away.

The newspapers began to report the deaths of anyone who might have had any connection with Carnarvon or the tomb, thereby linking further deaths with 'the curse'. The deaths recorded included those of Carnarvon's younger brother Aubrey Herbert, an X-ray specialist on his way to examine the royal mummy; Carter's right-hand man Arthur Mace (who was in fact already suffering from pleurisy before the tomb was discovered); the American railroad magnate George Jay Gould (who had visited the tomb, but was touring Egypt due to his ill health); an unnamed associate curator in the British Museum (who was said to have been labelling objects from the tomb, although there are no objects from Tutankhamun's tomb in the British Museum); and the French Egyptologist Georges Bénédite (who died as a result of a fall after visiting the tomb). The list of 'victims of the mummy's curse' goes on, but the American Egyptologist Herbert E. Winlock took great pleasure in compiling his own list with the more rational explanations of these people's deaths. Today, the discovery of Tutankhamun's tomb is remembered as much for the 'curse' as for the Egyptological significance of this great archaeological excavation.   ◆

▼ *The tombs of Ramesses IX and Tutankhamun at the time of their re-opening in 1922. The Valley of the Kings was known to the ancient Egyptians as* ta set aat *, 'the Great Place', or more informally, as* ta int, *'the Valley'.*

Museums with Egyptian Collections

Many centuries of plunder, exchange, archaeological excavation and universal fascination with Egyptology have resulted in the dispersal of ancient Egyptian artefacts and the accumulation of important collections throughout the world.

Australia
Melbourne National Gallery of Victoria
Sydney Australian Museum, Nicholson Museum of Antiquities, Ancient History Teaching Collection

Austria
Vienna Kunsthistorisches Museum

Belgium
Antwerp Museum Vleeshuis
Brussels Musées Royaux d'Art et d'Histoire
Liège Musée Curtius
Mariemont Musée de Mariemont

Brazil
Rio de Janeiro Museu Nacional

Canada
Montreal McGill University, Ethnological Museum, Museum of Fine Arts
Toronto Royal Ontario Museum

Cuba
Havana Museo Nacional

Czechoslovakia
Prague Náprstkovo Muzeum

Denmark
Copenhagen Nationalmuseet, Ny Carlsberg Glyptotek, Thorwaldsen Museum

Egypt
Alexandria Graeco-Roman Museum
Aswan Museum on the Island of Elephantine
Cairo Egyptian Museum
Luxor Luxor Museum
Mallawi Mallawi Museum
Minya Minya Museum

France
Avignon Musée Calvet
Grenoble Musée de Peinture et de Sculpture
Limoges Musée Municipal
Lyons Musée des Beaux-Arts, Musée Guimet
Marseilles Musée d'Archéologie
Nantes Musée des Arts Décoratifs
Orléans Musée Historique et d'Archéologie de l'Orléanais
Paris Bibliothèque Nationale, Louvre, Musée du Petit Palais, Musée Rodin
Strasbourg Institut d'Egyptologie
Toulouse Musée Georges Labit

Germany
Berlin Staatliche Museen: Ägyptisches Museum, Staatliche Museen: Papyrussammlung, Staatliche Museen: Preussischer Kulturbesitz,
Dresden Albertinum
Essen Folkwang Museum
Frankfurt-am-Main Liebieghaus
Hamburg Museum für Kunst und Gewerbe, Museum für Völkerkunde
Hanover Kestner-Museum
Heidelberg Ägyptologisches Institut der Universität
Hildesheim Roemer-Pelizaeus-Museum
Karlsruhe Badisches Landesmuseum
Leipzig Ägyptisches Museum
Munich Staatliche Sammlung: Ägyptischer Kunst
Tübingen Ägyptologisches Institut der Universität
Würzburg Martin von Wagner Museum der Universität

Greece
Athens National Museum

Hungary
Budapest Szépmüvészeti Múzeum

Ireland
Dublin National Museum of Ireland

Italy
Bologna Museo Civico
Florence Museo Archeologico
Mantua Museo del Palazzo Ducale
Milan Museo Archeologico
Naples Museo Nazionale
Palermo Museo Nazionale
Parma Museo Nazionale di Antichità
Rome Museo Barracco, Museo Capitolino, Museo Nazionale Romano delle Terme Diocleziane
Rovigo Museo dell'Accademia delle Concordi
Trieste Civico Museo di Storta ed Arte
Turin Museo Egizio

Vatican Museo Gregoriano Egizte
Venice Museo Archeologico del Palazze, Reale di Venezia

Japan
Kyoto University Archaeological Museum

Mexico
Mexico City Museo Nacional de Antropologia

Netherlands
Amsterdam Allard Pierson Museum
Leiden Rijksmuseum van Oudheden
Otterlo Rijksmuseum Kröller-Müller

Poland
Kraków Muzeum Naradowe
Warsaw Muzeum Narodowe

Portugal
Lisbon Fundação Calouste Gulbenkian

Russia
Leningrad State Hermitage Museum
Moscow State Pushkin Museum of Fine Arts

Spain
Madrid Museo Arqueológico Nacional

Sudan
Khartum Sudan Museum

Sweden
Linköping Östergöttlands Museum
Lund Kulturhistoriska Museet
Stockholm Medelhavsmuseet
Uppsala Victoriamuseum

Switzerland
Basel Museum für Völkerkunde
Geneva Musée d'Art et d'Histoire
Lausanne Musée Cantonal d'Archéologie et d'Histoire,
Musée Cantonal des Beaux-Arts
Neuchâtel Musée d'Ethnographie
Riggisberg Abegg-Stiftung

United Kingdom
Birmingham Birmingham Museum and Art Gallery
Bolton Bolton Museum and Art Gallery
Bristol City Museum and Art Gallery
Cambridge Fitzwilliam Museum

Dundee Museum and Art Gallery
Durham Durham University Oriental
Museum
Edinburgh Royal Museum of Scotland
Glasgow Art Gallery and Museum,
Burrell Collection, Hunterian Museum
Leicester Museum and Art Gallery
Liverpool Museum of Archaeology,
Classics and Oriental Studies
London British Museum, Horniman
Museum, Petrie Museum of Egyptian
Archaeology, Victoria and Albert Museum
Manchester Manchester Museum
Norwich Castle Museum
Oxford Ashmolean Museum of Art and Archaeology, Pitt
Rivers Museum
Swansea Swansea Museum

United States of America
Baltimore (Md.) Walters Art Gallery
Berkeley (Ca.) Robert H. Lowie Museum of Anthropology
Boston (Mass.) Museum of Fine Arts
Brooklyn (N.Y.) Brooklyn Museum
Cambridge (Mass.) Fogg Art Museum, Harvard University,
Semitic Museum, Harvard University
Chicago (Ill.) Field Museum of Natural History, Oriental
Institute Museum
Cincinnati (Ohio) Art Museum
Cleveland (Ohio) Museum of Art
Denver (Col.) Art Museum
Detroit (Mich.) Detroit Institute of Arts
Kansas City (Miss.) William Rockhill Nelson Gallery of Art
Los Angeles (Ca.) County Museum of Art
Minneapolis (Minn.) Institute of Arts Museum
New Haven (Conn.) Yale University Art Gallery
New York Metropolitan Museum of Art
Palo Alto (Ca.) Stanford University Museum
Philadelphia (Pa.) Pennsylvania University Museum
Pittsburgh (Pa.) Museum of Art, Carnegie Institute
Princeton (N.J.) University Art Museum
Providence (R.I.) Rhode Island School of Design
Richmond (Va.) Museum of Fine Arts
St Louis (Miss.) Art Museum
San Diego (Ca.) Museum of Man
San Francisco (Ca.) M. H. De Young Memorial Museum
San José (Ca.) Rosicrucian Museum
Seattle (Wash.) Art Museum
Toledo (Ohio) Museum of Art
Washington D.C. Smithsonian Institution
Worcester (Mass.) Art Museum

from the *Atlas of Ancient Egypt* by John Baines and Jaromir Malek

Suggested Further Reading

Adams, B., *Egyptian Mummies* (Shire, 1984)

Allen, J.P. et al., *Religion and Philosophy in Ancient Egypt* (New Haven, 1989)

Andrews, C., *Egyptian Mummies* (British Museum Press, 1984)

Andrews, C., *Amulets of Ancient Egypt* (British Museum Press, 1994)

Baines, J. & **Malek,** J., *Atlas of Ancient Egypt* (Phaidon, 1984)

Bierbrier, M., *The Tomb Builders of the Pharaohs* (British Museum Press, 1982)

Bleeker, C.J., *Egyptian Festivals, Enactments of Religious Renewal* (Leiden, 1967)

Bleeker, C.J., *Hathor and Thoth* (Leiden, 1973)

Borghouts, J.F., *Ancient Egyptian Magical Texts* (E.J. Brill, 1978)

Bowman, A.K., *Egypt after the Pharaohs* (Guild, 1986)

David, A.R., *A Guide to Religious Ritual at Abydos* (Warminster, 1980)

David, R., *The Pyramid Builders of Ancient Egypt* (Routledge and Kegan Paul, 1986)

Dodson, A., *Egyptian Rock-cut Tombs* (Shire, 1991)

Englund, G. (ed.), *The Religion of the Ancient Egyptians: Cognitive Structures and Popular Expressions* (Uppsala, 1989)

Fairman, H.W., *The Triumph of Horus* (Batsford, 1974)

Faulkner, R.O., *The Ancient Egyptian Pyramid Texts* (Oxford University Press, 1969)

Faulkner, R.O., *The Ancient Egyptian Coffin Texts* (2 vols) (Aris and Phillips, 1973, 1977, 1987)

Faulkner, R.O., *The Ancient Egyptian Book of the Dead* (British Museum Press, 1989)

Foster, J.L., *Hymns, Prayers and Songs, An Anthology of Ancient Egyptian Lyric Poetry* (Scholars Press, Atlanta, Georgia, 1995)

Frankfort, H., *Kingship and the Gods, a study of Near Eastern Religion as the Integration of Society and Nature* (University of Chicago Press, 1948)

Ghalioungui, P., *Medicine and Magic in Ancient Egypt* (London, 1963)

Gwyn-Griffiths, J., *Plutarch's De Iside et Osiride* (University of Wales, 1970)

Hart, G., *Egyptian Myths* (British Museum Press, 1990)

Hart, G., *A Dictionary of Egyptian Gods and Goddesses* (Routledge & Kegan Paul, 1986)

Herodotus, *The Histories* (Penguin, 1972)

Hornung, E., *Conceptions of God in Ancient Egypt: The One and the Many* (Routledge & Kegan Paul, 1983)

Iversen, E., *The Myth of Egypt and its Hieroglyphs in European Tradition* (Copenhagen, 1961)

Janssen, R.& J., *Growing Up in Ancient Egypt* (Rubicon, 1990)

Kemp, B.J., *Ancient Egypt: Anatomy of a Civilisation* (Routledge, 1989, reprint 1991)

Lehner, M., *The Complete Pyramids* (Thames & Hudson, 1997)

Lichtheim, M., *Ancient Egyptian Literature Vol. I-III* (University of California, 1973-80)

Meeks, D. & **Favard-Meeks,** C., *Daily Life of the Egyptian Gods* (London, 1996)

Morenz, S., *Egyptian Religion* (Methuen, 1973)

Nunn, J.F., *Ancient Egyptian Medicine* (British Museum Press, 1997)

Pinch, G., *New Kingdom Votive Offerings to Hathor* (Oxford, 1993)

Pinch, G., *Magic in Ancient Egypt* (British Museum Press, 1994)

Quirke, S., *Who were the Pharaohs?* (British Museum Press, 1990)

Quirke, S., *Ancient Egyptian Religion* (British Museum Press, 1992)

Quirke, S., *Hieroglyphs and the Afterlife in Ancient Egypt* (British Museum Press, 1996)

Redford, D.B., *Akhenaten: The Heretic King* (Princeton, 1984)

Reeves, N., *The Complete Tutankhamun* (Thames and Hudson, 1990)

Reeves, N. & **Wilkinson,** R.H., *The Complete Valley of the Kings* (Thames and Hudson, 1996)

Robins, G., *Women in Ancient Egypt* (British Museum Press, 1993)

Romer, J., *Ancient Lives* (Henry Holt and Co., 1984)

Sadek, A.I., *Popular Religion in Egypt during the New Kingdom* (Hildesheim, 1987)

Sauneron, S., *The Priests of Ancient Egypt* (Grove, 1960)

Shafer, B.E., (ed.), *Religion in Ancient Egypt* (Cornell, 1991)

Shaw, I. & **Nicholson,** P., *British Museum Dictionary of Ancient Egypt* (British Museum Press, 1995)

Snape, S. *Egyptian Temples* (Shire, 1996)

Spencer, A.J., *Death in Ancient Egypt* (Penguin, 1982)

Taylor, J.H., *Death and the Afterlife in Ancient Egypt* (British Museum Press, 1999)

Velde, H. te, *Seth, God of Confusion* (2nd edn) (1977)

Watson, P., *Egyptian Pyramids and Mastaba Tombs* (Shire, 1987)

Wildung, D., *Egyptian Saints: Deification in Pharaonic Egypt* (New York University Press, 1977)

Wilkinson, R.H., *Reading Egyptian Art: A Hieroglyphic Guide to Ancient Egyptian Painting and Sculpture* (Thames and Hudson, 1992)

Acknowledgements

AKG Photographic: p9 top (Agyptisches Museum, Berlin), 6–7, 18 bottom (Egyptian Museum, Cairo), 19 left, p28 (Louvre, Paris), p29 bottom (Louvre, Paris), p32 top, p32 bottom (Luxor Museum), p39 (British Museum, London), p41 top (Kunthistorisches Museum, Vienna), p45 bottom, 46 left, p54 top, p66 (National Maritime Museum, Haifa), p77 bottom (Egyptian Museum, Cairo), p83 bottom (Kunthistorisches Museum, Vienna), p88–89, p92 top, p100–101, p112 top, p115 (Louvre, Paris), p116

The Ancient Art & Architecture Collection: p10 bottom, p18 top, p36 bottom, 38 bottom, p58 top, p59 left, p64 left, p65 bottom, p67 top and bottom, p68, p71 right, p78 top

The Ancient Egypt Picture Library: p19 right, p20, p30 top, 38 top (Egyptian Museum, Cairo), p43,

p45 top, 47 top, p52 bottom, p56, p58 bottom, p62 bottom (Louvre, Paris), p64 right, p70 left, p80 bottom (British Museum, London), p84, p92 bottom, p94 bottom, p117 top

The Art Archive: p8 bottom, p12 bottom, p21 right (Egyptian Museum, Cairo), p22 (Egyptian Museum, Cairo), p29 top (Egyptian Museum, Cairo), p31, p34 top, 37 top (Egyptian Museum, Cairo), p42 top, p70 right (Egyptian Museum, Cairo), p71 left (Louvre, Paris), p94 top (Egyptian Museum, Cairo), p106 top, p110–111 (Luigi Mayer, 'Views in Egypt', 1801), p112 bottom (Antalya Museum), p114 top (British Museum), p117 bottom (Civic Museum, Turin)

The Bridgeman Art Library: p11 left (The Louvre, Paris), p12 top (Ashmolean Museum, Oxford), p21 left (Louvre, Paris), p23 left (Freud Museum, London), p23 right (Ashmolean Museum, Oxford), p33 bottom (British Museum), p35 top (Louvre, Paris), p40 top (Sir John Soane Museum, London), p40 bottom (Louvre, Paris), p41 bottom (British Museum, London), p42 bottom (Louvre, Paris), p46 right, p51 bottom (British Museum, London), p54 bottom (Fitzwilliam Museum, University of Cambridge), p57 (Stapleton Collection), p61 bottom (British Museum, London), p62 top (Freud Museum, London), p69 (Ashmolean Museum, Oxford), p74 top (Ashmolean Museum, Oxford), p74 bottom, p78 bottom (Giraudon), p80 top (British Museum, London), p82 (Fitzwilliam Museum, Cambridge), p85 bottom (Bode Museum, Berlin), p93, p95 bottom, p98, p99 top, p102 bottom (Fitzwilliam Museum, Cambridge), p103 (Louvre, Paris), p108 (Louvre, Paris), p109 right (Bonhams, London),

p113 (Museo Archeologico Prenestino, Palestrina), p118 top (The Illustrated London, News Picture Library, London)

C M Dixon: p27 right (National Museum, Florence)

Hulton Getty: p119 top and bottom

Lucia Gahlin: p11 right, p30 bottom, 35 bottom, p50, p87 top, p99 bottom

Michael Holford: p27 left (British Museum, London), p27 middle (British Museum, London), p33 top

Peter Clayton: p37 bottom, p52 top, p63, p72 top and bottom, p81, p83 top

Robert Harding: p8 top, p36 top (Egyptian Museum, Cairo), p53, p85 top, p87 bottom, p95 top

Sylvia Cordaiy Photo Library: p10 top, p104 top

Travel Ink: p16–17, p55, p73, p79

The Griffith Institute/Ashmolean Museum, Oxford: p118 bottom

Werner Forman Archive: p24 (Egyptian Museum, Cairo), p34 bottom (Egyptian Museum, Cairo), p47 bottom (Egyptian Museum, Cairo), p51 top (Schultz Collection, New York), p59 right (Egyptian Museum), p60, p61 top (courtesy L'Ibis, New York), p65 top, p75 (Archaelological Museum, Khartoum), p76 (E Strouhal), p77 top (Egyptian Museum, Cairo), p86, p102 top, p104 (Dr E Strouhal), p105 bottom left and right, p106 bottom (E Strouhal), p107 (Egyptian Museum, Cairo, p109 left (private collection), p114 bottom (Egyptian Museum, Cairo)

Index